SERENDIPITEA

SERENDIPITEA

A GUIDE TO THE VARIETIES, ORIGINS, AND RITUALS OF TEA

Tomislav Podreka

William Morrow and Company, Inc. / New York

It is the policy of William Morrow and Company, Inc., and its imprints and affiliates, recognizing the importance of preserving what has been written, to print the books we publish on acid-free paper, and we exert our best efforts to that end.

Library of Congress Cataloging-in-Publication Data

Podreka, Tomislav.
Serendipitea : a guide to the varieties, origins, and rituals of tea / Tomislav Podreka. — 1st ed.
p. cm.
Includes index.
ISBN 0-688-15808-0
1. Tea. 2. Tea—History. I. Title.
GT2905.P63 1998
641.3'372—dc21 98-6816
CIP

Printed in the United States of America

First Edition

1 2 3 4 5 6 7 8 9 10

BOOK DESIGN BY RICHARD ORIOLO

www.williammorrow.com

Klaudio Sr.,

thank you for encouraging me to think, and

Juljana,

thank you for reminding

me to laugh.

Linda,

at the right times you said the right

things and made this man.

Acknowledgments

Thank you to all my colleagues in the tea industry who have had to endure grueling cross-examinations on the nature of and details of tea. And thank you to Mary Goodbody, who with the fine support of Francine Fielding made this book into an enticing cup of information, well rounded, full of character, and refreshing.

My warmest thanks to my editor, Beccy Goodhart, for having patience and confidence in this book. Your gentle strength has been my guiding light. Great thanks to my agent, Katharine Sands, for recognizing a book and bringing me to William Morrow.

Thank you to all the people at William Morrow who I have had the pleasure to work with, including Carrie Weinberg and Corinne Alhadeff in publicity, Richard Aquan, the art director, Richard Oriolo for the book design, in the copyediting department, Kathy Antrim, Lisa Healy, and Virginia McRae—and, finally, to all those people in between who have contributed in some way to this book.

Contents

Introduction

No beverage has influenced the course of the world as much as tea. For centuries, it has been a key player in trade and commerce, building bridges between Europe and Asia, the New World and Europe, Asia and the Americas. What is more, how tea is steeped, served, and enjoyed has helped to establish a rich legacy of social mores and customs.

Today, if the world's billions of tea drinkers were to find themselves without it, they would be lost. Whether it is drunk with the morning toast, served as part of a ritualized Japanese tea ceremony, chatted over at an Afghan tea stand, served with scones and clotted cream in an elegant London hotel, or poured into a large glass pitcher and served iced and sweet at a southern roadhouse, tea is part of the culinary landscape the world over.

A Life of Tea

Since I spend most of my waking hours lecturing on tea and demonstrating its preparation, hardly a day goes by without my being asked how I know so much about it. The answer is simple, yet wonderfully enigmatic: I did not find out about tea. I have always known about it, although I may not have realized it.

My earliest memories of tea and comfort are one and the same. The tea, milky and sweet, was always there for me when I came home, even as a quite young boy. But it did not steep on its own, of course: Its appearance was the work of the central figure in my life, my mum. Psychologists tell us our sense of taste and smell are the most powerful markers of memory, so it is easy to understand why that warm cup of tea is one of the most enduring symbols of my mother's love. Security and routine are terribly important to children no matter where they live, and I knew that the simple act of returning home, walking through the kitchen door, and saying, "Hallo Mama, *kako si?* (how are you?)" would be followed with the sweet and comforting "cuppa."

My parents were Croatian immigrants who spoke very little English when they arrived in Australia, where I was born and raised. Like immigrants and travelers anywhere, they relied on alternative means to communicate with their new neighbors. Tea, being a familiar beverage to both immigrant and Australian, was an important part of our daily life, especially while my small family was establishing itself in its new home. When guests arrived, regardless of where they were from, tea was offered as a symbol of hospitality and friendship. Not offering tea would be taken as an obvious slight, and my mother could hardly bring the pot to the table fast enough.

Tea is one of the most universal symbols of hospitality. It announces a moment of peace, a time to collect our thoughts for gentle, quiet visits. Just as the shared pot helped new arrivals in our neighborhood in Australia feel at home, so it does the world over.

This was particularly true in the far-flung countries of the British Commonwealth, as I know from being a child growing up in Australia. It is also true of other cultures, which I will address later in the book. For me, it was its Englishness that defined tea. Whether one lived in Australia, Canada, or South Africa, a British thread ran through all aspects of quotidian life, and tea was an integral part of that shared culture. Whenever life got a little tough—the car broke down, the children were obstreperous—or when it became downright unbearable, a cup of tea was a way to prop oneself up. It was and always will be a positive force, a helping hand and symbol of kind comfort. It is a friend, a pick-me-up, and in the worst of times, the very thing to keep our upper lips stiff.

When I was a boy, I frequently rose before dawn to go fishing. My mother sent me off in the dark, cool morning with a thermos of hot tea and a bewildered but loving shake of her head: How could anyone *choose* to rise so early? Once ensconced on the dock, I quietly watched as the blood-red sun slipped gloriously over the horizon. When the first slivers of dawn's light reached me, I cracked the lid of the thermos. The aroma of tea liberally mixed with orange juice and sugar wafted up to greet me, beckoning me with warm, enticing fingers of steam. I barely realized I was honoring the daily sunrise with the tea, but looking back I realize I was performing a ritual of personally significant proportions. I admit now that I recall the fragrance of the tea more than the flavor because to this day I remember the unpleasant taste imparted by the plastic thermos cup!

When my brother and I were teenagers, my father insisted that we take up a martial art. He reasoned that the confidence and knowledge gained would stand us in good stead as we made our way through the world. Before studying several styles, I first studied tae kwon do. I remember the first master I worked with, a quiet Korean who instructed the class with a series of demonstrations and grunts before retiring to the side of the room to watch us work. He inevitably opened his blue-and-white thermos and poured hot tea into a white, handleless cup. For what seemed an eternity, he gazed into the cup before taking a single sip. I was intrigued by this repeated ritual—and amazed by how quickly he would leap to his feet to correct a pupil who was performing badly.

When studying kung fu a few years later with another master, my fellow students and I often went to a small Chinese restaurant after class. There we sat in a cramped upstairs room and drank tea while discussing our class and our lives. One day I asked the owner if he had any tea for us to try other than the standard house fare. He brought out five different types and set about explaining their distinctions in heavily accented, limited English with many hand gestures. I understood not a word, but my palate was elated. The next evening, a young man asked to work with me at the dojo, and as we went through our paces, I realized he was the restaurant owner's son. His father had asked him to translate for him should I want to know more about tea. I happily returned to the restaurant for an invaluable education.

Tea, this father-son team explained, was only as good as the use to which it was put. They compared it to kung fu, saying that if I studied only to keep in shape and for the physical exercise, the discipline would never go beyond being an empty sport. But if I opened my mind to the total experience, I could achieve astonishing feats. If I drank tea only as refreshment and for its health benefits, it would never be more than a bland, meaningless beverage. If, on the other hand, I searched for more, expected more from tea, I would find more. I came to understand that the importance of both kung fu and tea rested in how I applied the knowledge to my life—not in how others judged me.

Entering the Tea Business

I realize now that I grew to adulthood knowing about tea because I drank tea. It was an integral part of my life and, although I did not fully realize it, I cared deeply about well-made, good-tasting tea and what it meant to my overall well-being. It should be mentioned that there are no "degree" courses or certifying bodies to qualify one as a tea professional. Most tea specialists gain their expertise by working for a tea company or through their interest in tea.

As do many young men, I yearned to travel to the United States and managed to get a work visa based on my abilities as a ballroom-dancing coach. Once in New York, I discovered that I needed to supplement my dancing income with odd jobs, and so, in 1992, I began selling a line of natural remedy skin care products and essential oils at Barney's Apothecary, eventually leading to a job managing an art space at Felissimo in New York, which was adjacent to a tea room. I found myself advising customers on different teas, despite the fact that this was not my primary job. I enjoyed the exchange of information and inquirers were quite surprised and pleased to discover how much I knew about tea—and how firm my opinions were on the subject. This led to an approach from a fledgling tea company. My job was to help develop a line of teas and tisanes, as well as other tea-inspired products such as soaps, bath teas, and candles. I was happy to work with this start-up, but soon decided to strike out on my own and develop my own line of teas. Thus my company, serendipitea, was launched in 1994.

By this time I was married. My wife, Linda, and I spent all our evenings and weekends at Linda's mother's house, packing teas in the basement and using the kitchen table as a "cupping laboratory," the place where we steeped and tasted tea after tea, deciding which were best and met our exacting standards.

I knew from the start that we would sell only loose tea. No tea bags for serendipitea! But to make a go of it in the United States, I realized that Americans would require some education on the desirability of drinking freshly infused tea made from high-quality leaves.

Happily, the consumption of quality tea is catching on like wildfire in the United States and Canada, the latter having had historically a higher rate of tea consumption than its southern neighbor. Loose tea, handsomely packed, is finding its way into North American shops; the culinary pages of newspapers and magazines are filled with instructions for steeping a perfect cup and for using tea in recipes; and tea parlors and tea shops are popping up everywhere. Tea sales in the United States have grown significantly in recent years, with types such as green and oolong teas making real inroads into the market.

For me, and indeed for all tea lovers, this is marvelous news. As a tea merchant, I am pleased by the figures, but as a tea connoisseur, I feel strongly that we must understand and respect tea if we are to enjoy this ancient and sustaining drink to its fullest. That is why I have written this book—it is my love letter to the beverage that has meant so much to the world and to so many people in their public and private lives and, in the end, so much to me.

The History of Tea

Shrouded in myth and hazy facts, the origins of tea remain elusive. The lore invites us on a journey to exotic lands and ancient times, offering more romance than cold, clear proof. But this is how it should be: Much of the appeal of tea stems from our curiosity about how mankind first brought the remarkable beverage to his lips.

It is difficult to ascribe dates to ancient events, particularly to those surrounding something so widely enjoyed as tea. Most experts accept 2737 B.C. as the year when tea was first drunk, probably in what is now the Chinese province of Szechwan. As the story goes, the legendary emperor Shen Nung was strolling through his garden, drinking his customary cup of boiled water, when a leaf from a nearby bush drifted into his cup. Rather than fish it out, the emperor let the leaf

remain, watching with fascination as it tinted the clear water. He tried a sip—and declared it a refreshing drink, indeed. After experimenting with the tea, Shen Nung also declared tea a medicinal drink. He was a productive man who is credited with writing the *Pen ts'ao*, an early text on herbal medicine, among other intellectual pursuits. In reality, this text was most likely written much later, during the Han Dynasty, 206 B.C. to A.D. 221. (In addition, the emperor is credited with inventing the plow and introducing animal husbandry to his people; his name translates literally as "divine husbandman.") Whether Shen Nung is more than a legend is debatable, but there is evidence of an ancient hill tribe called Shen-nung, which is credited with advances in agriculture.

Later, Taoist philosopher Lao-tzu, while on his Great Western Journey through Szechwan in the sixth century B.C., was offered a bowl of tea by a student. This small story is significant because it indicates further evidence of the province's place as the cradle of tea. But more important, it establishes an early standard of etiquette, that of presenting tea as a gesture of hospitality.

Another legend tells of India's Prince Siddhartha "discovering" tea in that country at approximately the same time that Lao-tzu was living. While attempting to meditate, the story goes, the young prince

instead fell asleep. Upon waking, he was so frustrated and disgusted by his weakness that he tore off his eyelids and tossed them angrily to the ground. Amazingly, from these grew a shrub with leaves that, when infused as tea, held great properties of mental clarity. Without doubt, this is the stuff of legends. In Japan a similar story exists, but in that island nation it is said that it was Daruma (Bodhidharma) whose eyelids became the tea shrub. Despite the different versions of the tale, the message remains the same: Tea has long been considered a beverage that sharpens the mind's eye. To this day, there is a Chinese tea called "eyelid tea."

Regardless of whether tea shrubs were actually growing from eyelids, by 500 B.C. the people of Asia were drinking and benefiting from tea. Another contemporary of Siddhartha wrote, "Who can say that tea is bitter? It is as sweet as the shepherd's purse." Written by none other than Confucius, these words ring with truth. Some historians actually credit Confucius with being the father of tea, and it is commonly claimed that this most practical of all men extolled the virtues of *tu* (tea) as a means of ensuring that the Chinese people drank their water boiled and thus prevented the spread of disease. Alas, no written proof of this sensible philosophy exists, but it is too splendid a piece of Chinese oral history to ignore.

Tea in Asia

The first reliable reference to tea comes from an ancient Chinese dictionary written around A.D. 350. It describes tea (by now pronounced *cha*) primarily as a medicinal beverage prepared by boiling raw green tea leaves in kettles of water. This was common practice among the hill dwellers of southwest China, and had Confucius tasted the concoction, he might have revised his opinion of tea downward. Although imbibers must have recognized that somehow the bitter brew warded off illness, it was undoubtedly a nasty-tasting drink.

During this time, the Chinese actively began cultivating the tea plant, *Camellia sinensis*. Not only did the cultivated plant produce a pleasant-tasting tea, but horticulturists also discovered that its leaves could be stripped without killing the entire plant. It is significant to note that well into the nineteenth century, *only* the Chinese understood how to cultivate tea plants, a fact that gave them great financial advantages for generations, but also ultimately led to the devastation of the Opium Wars.

It took generations of tea drinking before the next great leap in tea production was made: The Chinese processed tea leaves by pressing them into cakes, which were roasted and pounded and then broken into small pieces for infusion. To improve further upon the flavor of the tea, ginger and onions were sometimes added to the mix.

By this time, the end of the fifth century A.D., tea had become an important article of commerce, even though it was still drunk mainly as a medicinal herb. Mongols bartered it with Turkish traders, who carried it far from its Chinese origins.

The Chinese next began producing bricks of tea, which quickly became valued currency in remote regions of the country and greatly accelerated the spread of tea. The bricks were made by pounding the tea leaves and then pressing them into molds that were dried over heat. The bricks were easy to carry and efficient to use. It is quite possible that when these valuable bricks were traded and a celebratory cup of tea was shared among traders, a variation of the phrase "Let's drink to your wealth—and to your health" was born.

When tea became currency, it shrugged off its medicinal robes entirely and evolved into a beverage of distinction and refreshment. It was celebrated in the ancient arts—whether in poetry or pottery—and, as a crowning glory, was granted its own Chinese character. (Prior to this time, the ideogram for tea might have been the same used for sow thistle or even common grass.)

In A.D. 780, the Chinese began taxing tea. Demand for it was growing, and the Chinese realized the tax would provide a steady revenue stream from the outer reaches of the country and beyond. The tax reached Tibet and other areas inhabited by nomadic tribes such as Turks, Tatars, and Mongols, all of whom clamored for tea and were willing to pay for the privilege of buying it.

In the same year, a Taoist named Lu Yu wrote ten slim volumes called the *Ch'a Ching* (*The Classic of Tea*), which melded tea and Taoism, reflecting the spirit of the times and promising peace, harmony, and balance through the use of tea. In addition, the *Ch'a Ching* covered aspects such as sowing the plant, harvesting its leaves, making tea, and serving it. The books set standards for the critical evaluation of tea, while reminding the reader that "its goodness is a decision for the mouth to make."

Although Lu Yu frowned on adding onions, ginger, and other herbs to tea, he advocated adding salt, a practice that reduced the bitterness and provided an almost sweet taste. This was sound advice, since so much of the tea brewed in those times was steeped far too long and was, by all accounts, dark and unpleasantly bitter.

By now the Chinese were making tea in three forms: cakes, powder, and leaves. The cake remained the favorite among connoisseurs, who broke off just the amount they desired, ground it to a fine powder, and then poured boiling water over it. Powdered tea was similar, but considered not quite as fine, since it was not hand-ground by the tea lover. Leaf tea tended to spoil, and so was the least popular; it would still be some time before methods for drying and storing it were perfected.

During the Song Dynasty, which lasted from A.D. 960 to 1280, the Chinese favored delicate teas made from fine powders, which, once brewed, where whisked to a froth. Occasionally, fragrant flowers such as jasmine and roses were blended with the tea, making subtle infusions that inspired poetic names. The mid-dynasty emperor Huei Tsung allegedly preferred tea leaves that were snipped by virgins with gold scissors and spread on gold platters to dry, a custom that came to be known as "imperial plucking." So enamored of tea was Huei that he wrote a book called *Ta Kuan Ch'a Lun* encouraging readers to persevere in the search for the ultimate cup of tea. Today's tea names such as Temple of Heaven and Dragon's Well are descendants of this era in Chinese history when poetry and refinement were all-important. It is interesting to note that the village of Dragon's Well still exists in China and is at the center of one of the country's tea-producing regions celebrated for its first-rate green tea.

Tea played a role outside court, too. Taoists claimed that it was an important ingredient in the elixir of immortality, despite the Tang poet Lu Tung's somewhat obsessive words: "I am in no way interested in immortality, but only in the taste of tea." Zen Buddhists sipped tea in their temples before images of Bodhidharma.

Although tea was served in Japan as early as the eighth century, it was not until the twelfth century that it acquired an association with Buddhism, which elevated its status considerably. While studying in China, a Zen Buddhist monk named Eisai observed tea's increasingly important role in temple ceremonies and determined to return to Japan with the seeds for tea plants. His instincts were right, for soon after his return to Japan, tea was incorporated into daily temple rites throughout Japan and very quickly found its way into the hearts of all Japanese.

Just as tea drinking was spreading across Japan, so was it affecting every aspect of daily life in China. With the establishment of the Ming Dynasty in 1368, drinking black, green, and oolong teas became popular with royalty and commoners alike. Loose-leaf tea came into its own during this time, as tea merchants discovered ways to keep it stable, thus making it safe to transport. It was at that time, too, that ceramic and porcelain teapots and elegant cups became objects of desire and prestige. The familiar round teapot, whose shape persists today, was modeled in the shape of a musk melon, said to be the best configuration for tea steeping, because it allows the water to flow, unimpeded by corners.

East Meets West

When tea was introduced in the West at the dawn of the seventeenth century, the world changed. It arrived on Dutch East India Company trade ships, carrying a cargo that the tea merchants had purchased in Japan. The Dutch proclaimed to their European customers that this was the finest tea China could produce. The truth of the matter was that the xenophobic Chinese refused to trade directly with the Europeans, and so used the Japanese as middlemen. Ironically, early shipments were probably Japanese green tea, not Chinese tea—but who knew or cared?

The Dutch were not the first Europeans to taste tea; this distinction most likely goes to Portuguese missionaries in Macao. But it was the Dutch who initiated its importation. Europe was ready, having for years heard of the "elixir of the East" from Arabs who controlled the overland trade routes.

Japan's global presence as a tea trader inspired the Chinese to expand their own trade routes. Quite early in the seventeenth century, Chinese tradesmen presented Russian Czar Alexis with several chests of tea, which he shared with his court. By the end of the century, transcontinental trade routes were established to supply Russia with tea. The trip was long and arduous, requiring caravans with up to three hundred camels to deliver enough tea for the noble class. The tea was carried in chests perched high on the camels' humps to keep it as far as possible from the animals' odiferous hides. Nevertheless, after months of travel and smoky nightly campfires, the tea assumed its own peculiar flavor unlike anything in China and came to be known as Russian caravan tea, the likes of which cannot be replicated—perhaps this is just as well—although today a blend of pleasing smoky tea carries the romantic name of Russian Caravan tea or Caravan tea.

The first public offering of tea took place at Thomas Garraway's shop in central London in 1657. A decade or so later, the English East India Company persuaded the British government to ban Dutch imports, which led to a monopoly for the company and significant smuggling activities by the Dutch.

The New World should not be overlooked during this century of rapid expansion for the tea trade. Tea was first brought to New Amsterdam (later New York) by the Dutch in the mid-seventeenth century, and within a few years, the population of Manhattan Island was said to consume more tea than the entire population of the British Isles.

The End of China's Dominance

By the beginning of the eighteenth century, the vast tea trade was dominated by the English, Dutch, and French, although soon the

English would have a complete monopoly. The Chinese were having trouble keeping up with demand. They began exporting inferior tea, a practice that the English found intolerable. Lord Macartney, a British viscount and diplomat, was dispatched to China to remedy the situation, but once on Chinese shores discovered that the job was close to impossible. Why? The English had nothing the Chinese wanted to trade for tea except silver. Essentially at the mercy of the Chinese, the British had no choice but to load their ships with silver and send them off to China. With great frequency the ships were commandeered by pirates, who made off with the silver, making the tea trade even more expensive than it already was.

The financial woes of the tea trade and the East India Company prompted the British government to enact the Tea Act in 1773, which enabled the faltering company to sell tea at reduced prices in North America. English tea merchants were desperate to compete with the Dutch, who smuggled so much tea into the New World that the English imports dwindled from 320,000 pounds in 1769 to 530 pounds in 1772. It also put the English government in league with the East India Company, which resulted in tea trading in the colonies being handled mainly by loyalists. Although the Tea Act did not directly impose a tea tax on the colonies, it galled them, in particular the Sons of Liberty whose ranks included Samuel Adams and Paul Revere. This unrest resulted in the Boston Tea Party in December of 1773—a pivotal event leading to the American Revolution. "Boston Harbor: A teapot tonight!" was the rallying cry that went up at Boston's old South Church on that fateful day.

With silver proving an impractical medium of exchange and the Tea Act proving disastrous to trade, the English East India Company turned to a commodity the Chinese wanted: opium. Addiction to opium throughout China (and, to a lesser extent, throughout England and the United States) was astoundingly rapid. Soon, the British East India Company was reaping the financial rewards of trading opium for tea, albeit through smaller companies called Free Traders, which acted as fronts. These tacitly sanctioned drug dealers carried Indian opium from open-trade markets in Calcutta to the ports of China.

This, too, was the brief but highly romanticized era of sleek clipper ships, an American nautical innovation which plied the waters between England, India, China, the United States, and Australia, carrying tea and opium—although tea was the only cargo much talked about in most circles in Europe. By the 1860s, steamships made the sailing vessels obsolete, but their image and appeal persisted.

The British oversaw the production and sale of opium in India, but once it left the subcontinent's shores with the Free Traders bound for China where it was exchanged for tea, they washed their hands of it. With highly evolved twentieth-century–style denial, the English were able to persuade themselves that the East India Company had nothing to do with the drug trade. When the Chinese revolted against the ruin that widespread drug addiction wrecked on its populace, many Londoners chose to call this the Burmese War rather than the Opium Wars. As it turned out, the Opium Wars were a disaster for the Chinese, who could not compete with English firepower. The 1841 Treaty of Nanking signaled the end to the armed skirmishes and the end of the powerful Chinese tea trade. It also granted Britain a small peninsula of land called Hong Kong, among other things.

"Direct from the Tea Garden to the Teapot"

Thomas Lipton was an enterprising Scot who, even before he was forty, owned a chain of three hundred general stores in his homeland. Eager to stock tea on his stores' shelves, Lipton traveled to Ceylon in 1890, where he purchased four estates at very low prices because of the recent demise of the coffee plantations in that country. Lipton planted tea on his land and went into the business with characteristic enthusiasm.

Lipton's ideas and energy soon infused tea production on his estates, which he modernized by introducing the rolling machines invented by another Scot, James Taylor, and dryers. He was able to undersell other tea merchants in England and it wasn't long before he expanded his business to the United States and Canada. Lipton, who had spent a few years in New York during his youth, had mastered the American talent for advertising and promotion, using slogans such as "Direct from the tea garden to the teapot" and "The perfect tea to suit the water of your town." These skills, combined with his extensive knowledge of the product, made him a household word in Europe and the Americas—and his name remains so today.

Realizing that the days of Chinese tea trading were over, the English began raising tea in India. During the days of the Raj, the English worked hard to establish tea estates in India, making sub-rosa forays into China to glean information and lure the Chinese from their homeland to run the Indian plantations. Fortuitously, *Camellia assamica*, a wild tea plant, was discovered growing in the Assam region of northern India, a discovery that led to the establishment of the Assam Company and attracted Englishmen seeking their fortunes to India.

Soon, tea was also being cultivated in Ceylon (now Sri Lanka). It was in Ceylon that Scotsman Thomas Lipton began his first plantation. And so, by the close of the nineteenth century, Europeans and Americans associated tea far more readily with India and Ceylon than with China, which represented a major change in global consciousness. For more than two hundred years, the words "tea" and "China" had been nearly synonymous, but those days were over. Tea could be produced in other lands with equally flavorful results.

Today, tea is enjoying a resurgence, particularly in the West, where the United States is on the verge of creating new tea traditions of its own.

On the Tea Estates

We drink Darjeeling, Earl Grey, green, Jasmine, and oolong teas, rarely considering the vast differences among them, much less what these names mean. In countries such as the United States, where most tea is the watery product of an inexpensive tea bag or an iced drink made from (give me strength!) sweetened crystallized powder, it's no wonder that the rich and varied world of tea is overlooked—sometimes to the point of ignorance of its very existence.

I recall my first experience with tea upon arriving in the United States. Feeling a little homesick and lonely, I stopped by a coffee shop and ordered a cup of tea. I was presented with a small pot of not-quite-boiling water and an empty cup and saucer with a tea bag carelessly tossed on the side. I wrote this off to a poor choice of restaurant on my part as an uninformed newcomer. But I grew increasingly dismayed and alarmed as the experience repeated itself time and again. I soon discovered this was the custom in the United States. In upscale restaurants, I was offered a selection of tea bags—but never was the tea made as it should be. This shameful situation is one that I and other tea lovers are working to change. To paraphrase a wise Chinese adage, a long journey begins with the first step, and the first step in this journey is to educate everyone who appreciates tea, but knows very little about it.

The Tea Plant

Exploring the world of tea is a fascinating adventure and one that begins with the cultivation and harvest of the plant itself. It may surprise many to learn that all tea comes from the same plant, *Camellia sinensis*. Where it is grown and how it is processed determines the type of tea. Both the Chinese tea plant and its cousin, the wild Assam tea plant, which was discovered growing in India's Upper Assam region in the nineteenth century, are *Camellia sinensis*, albeit different varieties of the same genus. The Assam plant is a subspecies called *Camellia assamica*.

The original Chinese plant, cultivated for centuries in its native country, is smaller and more cold-resistant with smaller, rounder leaves than Assam tea. The Assam tea plant can grow to be thirty feet tall, has larger leaves, and produces a darker, more intensely flavored tea. Although it grows more prolifically, the Assam plant is more sensitive to the cold. For generations, the tea plant was believed to be indigenous only to China and Assam, but we now know that it is native to Myanmar (Burma), Cambodia, Vietnam,

Laos, Thailand, and Tibet, too. (In Myanmar and Cambodia, the variety is called *Camellia assamica lasiocalyx.*)

Over time, the two plant varieties have been cross-cultivated for hybrids of varying size and sturdiness. Not surprisingly, tea plants with more of the characteristics of the original Chinese plant are grown in China, Taiwan, and Japan, while those with the characteristics of the Assam plant are grown in India, Sri Lanka, Australia, South America, and Africa. Naturally there are exceptions to these generalities.

Tea is grown in more than forty countries, although most aficionados agree that the best teas in the world come from only five: China, Japan, Taiwan, India, and Sri Lanka. Also worth noting are Kenya, Malawi, Indonesia, Turkey, and Argentina, for the great quantities exported.

Tea Cultivation

Nearly all the tea in the world is cultivated. Very little of it is picked in the wild, although a few hill tribes in Southeast Asia still pluck leaves from bushes growing along mountain ridges. Tea is grown on estates or plantations of varying sizes, many of them extending as far as the eye can see, with acre upon acre undulating with soft green, carefully placed, and meticulously pruned bushes. The plants are never allowed to grow higher than about three feet, so that the young leaves can be harvested easily. When properly cared for, a tea plant will produce leaves for a century.

Tea prefers tropical or subtropical climates with ample rainfall and an altitude of at least one thousand and no more than seven thousand feet above sea level; the best teas are from plants grown above four thousand feet. The Chinese tea plants (*Camellia sinensis*) can survive cool, dry winters but require long and warm rainy seasons every year. Tea grows in sandy, loamy soil and can grow, indeed thrive, in soil that is too poor to sustain other crops. Depending on the climate, tea plants are harvested three or more times a year, with some harvested year-round.

Most fine tea is harvested by hand, although some mechanization is creeping into the industry. Still, the finest teas are those that are hand-plucked. Throughout Asia, women have been the traditional harvesters, in part because of their dexterity and smaller hands and also because men are needed for heavier labor on the tea estates, such as tilling the soil, planting and pruning the bushes, and packing the tea. The women arrive at the tea estates early in the morning toting wicker baskets, which are designed to hang from their backs and which they skillfully fill with leaves as they move along the rows of lush, green tea plants. A bamboo marker indicates how high on the bush the leaves should be plucked, which guards against overpicking.

Tea is picked so to include leaves and buds. These are not flower buds, but rather small furled leaves called buds. The buds are the most tender and flavorful form of the leaf, and teas made exclusively from buds are the rarest and finest. When a tea includes "tips," the reference is to the buds. Tea leaves either are "fine plucked" or "coarse plucked." Fine-plucked teas are from small shoots at the topmost section of the tea bush and include a bud and two leaves; coarse-plucked teas are from slightly larger shoots with three or more larger leaves. The best teas are from fine pluckings.

Processing Tea

From these leaves come all teas. How the leaves are handled after plucking determines the kind of tea they will become. First, however, the leaves are withered, which means they are spread out and allowed to dry naturally. All teas except most green tea and white tea are rolled, a process that releases the naturally occurring juices in the tea leaves, with the exception of Taiwanese oolongs, which are basket tossed. The leaves are then processed to become one of eight types of tea, which in turn may be blended into any of the hundreds of different blends. The eight types of tea are: black *pu'erh*, black (red), oolong, pouchong, green, yellow, white, and scented. However, not all tea experts agree with this breakdown. Some would not include pouchong, for instance, and others might not include yellow tea, but I feel this list is the most complete and describes tea as I know it.

Green and white teas are made from the withered leaves of the plants. All other teas are also fermented. Black teas are fully fermented, while pouchong and oolong are only partially fermented, with oolong being more fermented than pouchong. Oolong tea may be 75 percent fermented, while pouchong is usually 15 percent or less fermented. Both green and white teas are steamed immediately after withering to retard the enzymes that react with oxygen and result in fermentation. The steaming insures that these teas will not oxidize. Scented teas are made from green, oolong, or, most often, pouchong teas and are scented with a fragrance (jasmine springs easily to mind; for more on scented teas, see below).

Pu'erh is a rare black tea and may be in leaf form or compressed into cakes. It makes very strong and earthy-tasting tea. (For more on

Scented Tea

I list scented tea as a type of tea because it hails from an honorable and ancient tradition that began in China. Scented teas are not to be confused with flavored teas—those teas tagged as lemon- or cinnamon-flavored, for instance, or even the honorable Earl Grey.

Scented teas are gently scented with the aroma of flower petals to become Jasmine or Rose teas. This is done with lightly fermented tea leaves, usually pouchong tea leaves that have not been heated to set the essential juices. The leaves are mixed with fresh flower petals, left for a prescribed period of time, and then separated from the petals. This process is repeated thirteen times, each time with fresh flower petals, until the tea is declared yin hao *or done. Superior scented teas have no flower petals left among the tea leaves. However, in modern times, it has become fashionable to leave a few petals to indicate that the teas were processed authentically. It also looks pretty.*

Pu'erh tea, see page 28.) All other black teas are known in Asia as red teas, a designation easily understood when you think of the color of the infused tea. In the West, red tea is called black tea, and so, except when I otherwise specify, I will call these teas black tea.

In the literal sense, tea leaves are not fermented, but rather are oxidized so that the flavors mellow and the aroma develops—but the term *fermentation* is part of the lexicon of tea producing and so stays firmly in place. This process occurs in cool rooms with high levels of humidity. Depending on the size of the tea factory, these rooms may be quite large. The rolled leaves are spread on large, flat surfaces to a depth of about an inch and left for several hours or less. Pouchong teas may require only twenty or thirty minutes of fermentation, while black teas may need as long as three hours.

When the leaves are fermented to the degree necessary for the type of tea, they are heated, or fired, to stop the oxidizing. At this point, the essential juices in the leaves are held in suspension and not released again until they are hydrated with boiling water at the time of infusion.

Most tea is grown, picked, sorted, processed, and packed on the tea estate. The buildings used for withering, fermenting, drying, and packing are referred to as the factory. I mention this only because when you hear of a "tea factory," the term does not pertain to large, industrial buildings, but airy and clean structures nestled in the midst of lovely green tea bushes.

Grades of Tea

Once the leaves are processed, they are graded. Just as wine has graded designations, so does tea. Although grades establish the type and quality of tea, they describe the appearance of the tea leaf and nothing more. However, since the condition of the leaf—whether a leaf is whole or torn, broken into many small pieces or reduced to dust—determines the quality of the tea, this is both sensible and important.

Pu'erh Tea

Pu'erh *teas are black teas most commonly found in China. They can be loose-leaf teas or compressed teas, but the defining element is their age, bacteria, and slight state of rot. During withering, some of the tea leaves are permitted to rot, thus the presence of bacteria. Next, the leaves are buried in the ground or, traditionally, aged in caves, for a period of time, which can be years, and then dug up and sold. The Chinese, Tibetans, Mongols, and others value this extremely strong, earthy tea, which smells and tastes of the soil.*

When pu'erh *tea is brewed, or steeped, it is nearly black and looks more like coffee than most people's idea of reddish, golden, or green-hued tea. It is nearly always served with milk, which cuts its strength. Tibetans are said to "cook" the tea all night and then, come morning, mix it with yak butter into a thick but highly prized drink. I have never tried this, but hear that it quickly becomes almost addictive. Mongols have historically mixed their* pu'erh *with mare's milk.*

The grades are recognized by a series of initials that to the uninitiated can be mind-boggling. I don't suggest memorizing these or even spending much time worrying about them. A quick explanation should suffice. Also, in the United States, the Food and Drug Administration (FDA) does not require any grading designations on tea, so understanding the coding system is not always useful. However, most tea merchants dealing in quality teas rely on the cod-

Compressed pu'erh *tea is consumed far more in China and other Asian countries than in Western countries. However, it is gaining in popularity here in a small way. The compressed cakes hark back to ancient days when the Chinese pressed tea leaves into bricks for transport into the far reaches of Asia. Today, I market a compressed tea called* tuo-cha, *which, when steeped, I mix with hot milk.*

Cakes of compressed tea are sold in Chinese groceries, but more often are found in Chinese herb shops and are admired for medicinal purposes. This is due to the presence of certain naturally occurring bacteria in the cakes. When the bricks are heated, or fired, the final time, a process that stabilizes the essential juices, the heat affects only the outer portions of the cake; if the heat were fierce enough to penetrate to the core, it would burn the outside. Bacteria develop in the core, and as the leaves are peeled from the core, the bacteria enter the tea.

ing system, and you will find it on the chests of the tea they sell. I put these codes on the teas I package, in particular Darjeeling, Ceylon, Assam, and Yunnan teas. As a rule, the codes are not found on Chinese or Japanese teas or on flavored teas.

When tea leaves are processed, many of them break into tiny pieces called fannings. The only level of tea *inferior* to a fanning is dust. Tea-leaf dust is used for poor-quality tea bags and, as far as I am concerned, merits very little attention. Fannings also find their way into tea bags and are superior to dust in terms of flavor and aroma. When the initial F appears at the end of a series of capital letters on a box or tin of tea, it refers to fannings; when the initial D appears, it refers to dust.

Other initials to look for are CTC, which refer to those black tea leaves that are cut in a specially designed machine. The machine's initials stand for crushing, tearing, and curling because that is precisely what happens to these leaves as they pass through the CTC. Now, here is a fresh conundrum for the tea drinker: These leaves make quite good-tasting tea with rich, deep color, but they are not considered high-quality leaves and in turn do not produce the *best* tea. What is going on? How can CTC teas be considered good-tasting but not high quality?

The answer is purely practical. Because the leaves are torn and crushed, the essential flavors in CTC leaves are quickly released when infused in boiling water and produce a full-flavored brew. They tint the water with color very quickly, too. For this reason, they can improve the characteristics of otherwise ordinary tea leaves. For the same reason, these leaves often are used for "gourmet tea bags." (I put quotation marks around the words "gourmet tea bags" because I personally feel there is no such thing. All tea bags are a waste of good tea and of your time.) As with all epicurean matters, whether you prefer teas labeled CTC to other teas—or whether you accept them at all—is a matter of personal taste.

Before I continue, I must address the word *pekoe*. The Chinese word *pak-ho* roughly means "white or light down," or, as some experts say, literally refers to the soft fuzz on a newborn baby's bot-

Blue Tea

In the old days, some teas were called blue tea because when mixed with boiling water, they literally turned blue. How odd, you might think! Blue tea was made from poor-quality oolong tea that was cut with gypsum powder, which explains the tint. The Chinese sold it to the unsuspecting Europeans and consequently, in the earliest days of the tea trade, it became the rage in some stylish European circles. Blue tea did not taste very good, but of course the Europeans had so little experience with tea then that they simply were charmed by its color and its mystique. Today, a few oolongs are labeled as blue teas, but these are quite often fancy oolongs and in most cases are made from very fine tea.

tom. The old-fashioned meaning for pekoe, then, refers to the downy substance on the bud. But as the language of tea has evolved, the term now refers to the second leaf on the shoot of a fine plucking.

Orange pekoe leaves have nothing to do with the color orange or the flavor of the citrus fruit. The term, derived from a reference to the princes of Orange, was most likely used by Dutch tea traders to indicate fancy tea. Today, orange pekoe refers to the larger of the leaves on a fine plucking and the term indicates a generally good-quality tea and would certainly not fit in a tea bag!

The best grade of tea is whole leaf tea. These teas are designated by a series of initials that frequently include the letter P, for pekoe. For example, the initials PS refer to Pekoe Souchong. Souchong leaves are the third leaves on the shoot and therefore from a coarse plucking and not considered as good as orange pekoe leaves.

The best grades of leaf tea are judged by the size and fullness of the twisted leaf and the lack of stem (except for Taiwanese oolong tea leaves, which commonly have stems). Good teas are also judged by the brightness of the leaf's color and the presence of buds. When the tea contains buds, words such as *golden*, *tippy*, *tip*, and *flowery* indicate their desirable presence.

The grade FOP refers to very good leaf tea; the initials stand for Flowery Orange Pekoe. This indicates that the tea is made from fine pluckings with just the right amount of bud and tender leaf tips. From here the grades go up, through GFOP (Golden Flowery Orange Pekoe), TGFOP (Tippy Golden Flowery Orange Pekoe), FTGFOP (Finest Tippy Golden Flowery Orange Pekoe), finally to SFTGFOP (Special Finest Tippy Golden Flowery Orange Pekoe)! You can see how quickly this becomes esoteric.

To seemingly add to the confusion, although in reality to clarify the system, the initials BPS stand for Broken Pekoe Souchong. BP refers to Broken Pekoe and BOP refers to Broken Orange Pekoe. True BOP is very good tea indeed, as it is made from broken orange pekoe leaves, with only the top halves of the leaves being used. However, as I said earlier, it is not as important to recognize these gradings as it is to be aware of their existence.

The Types of Tea Around the World

Tea is cultivated in more than forty countries, but as I mentioned earlier, nearly all connoisseurs agree that the best teas are produced in just five. Considering the history of tea, it comes as no surprise that these are China, Japan, Taiwan (which used to be called Formosa), India, and Sri Lanka (which used to be called Ceylon). Excellent teas come from other countries, of course, and as advances develop in cultivation and production, these teas only get better.

The tea plant was first cultivated centuries ago in China, and from those ancient tea estates came the world's first teas. This agricultural effort gave rise to what became one of our major commodities. Today, as always, far more people drink tea than drink coffee—in fact, tea is a close second to water as the world's most commonly consumed beverage—and as we enter the twenty-first century, the tea business is exploding with expanding markets, including a small and healthy specialty market.

Most tea is not sold as premium tea. The majority is the ordinary tea drunk daily from London to Bombay with such casual acceptance that tea drinkers think little about its qualities. Some people are fortunate enough to live in places where the tea sold for everyday consumption is first-rate; others are not so lucky and content themselves with weakly flavored hot water.

But as with anything that is commonly consumed, such as coffee, cheese, bread, and chocolate, there are vast degrees of difference in quality, and once you discover the "good stuff," it is hard to return to the mediocre. If you appreciate the difference between supermarket preground coffee and freshly ground French roast coffee, between processed American cheese and a fine Vermont Cheddar, between presliced store-bought white bread and a home-baked whole grain loaf, between an inexpensive candy bar and French Valrhona bittersweet chocolate, then I maintain you will also appreciate the difference between weak tea brewed from a cheap tea bag and a full-bodied, freshly steeped cup of Darjeeling leaf tea.

This is my mission: to educate tea drinkers about the great wealth of teas grown and blended in this world. Once you try good tea, you will never go back to mass-market tea bags and, like me, will feel cheated when fine restaurants insist on bringing hot water and tea bags when you order a cup of tea. Would they bring hot water and instant coffee?

Join me on a trip around the world to the tea-producing countries to learn about the various teas available. Listed here is a good cross-section of some of the best and most popular, two categories that may or may not be mutually exclusive. At first you may be confused. Some of the teas are named after a particular tea-growing estate or geographical region while others are named for a person, a plant, or a dimly remembered legend. Please accept this as it is and, as I do, glory in the idiosyncrasies of tea. It is an ancient beverage that over the centuries has been called everything from a mystical elixir to a scourge on those addicted to it. The teas listed here fall somewhere in between.

China

China is well respected for its long history of tea production. Early records of tea production are nonexistent, so we must rely on legend, but what is indisputable is that tea was cultivated here centuries before it was grown anywhere else. This heritage gives rise to some of the finest subtleties in the industry; it also makes China the country with the largest variety of teas. Tea is produced in seventeen principle regions, which are Anhui, Fujian, Gansu, Guangdong, Guangxi Zhuang, Guizhou, Hainan, Henan, Hubei, Hunan, Jiangsu, Jiangxi, Shaanxi, Shandong, Szechwan, Yunnan, and Zhejiang.

The Chinese drink mainly green tea, but export mainly black tea. Up until the Second World War and the advent of communism in China, the Chinese exported more than half the world's tea; today they export about 6 percent.

When infused, black tea tints the water a reddish color, the hue most familiar to Westerners when they think of tea. This is why throughout Asia, black tea often is called "red tea." It is also sometimes called *Congou* tea, a reference to traditionally fermented, hand-fired Chinese teas. As explained earlier in the discussion of processing tea (page 25), black tea is fermented, or oxidized. Oolong tea is black tea that has not been permitted to oxidize to the same extent as other black teas. The Chinese produce fine oolongs by rolling the long slender tea leaves until they break and then oxidizing them only minimally.

When searching for new and intriguing Chinese teas, remember that not everything is in a name. When Mao Zedong succeeded in taking control of China, the only office he left in place from the old regime was the Tea Board. The board's sole responsibility was to create names for teas—in effect to market the same teas over and over again under different names.

BLACK TEAS

Lapsang Souchong: This strong, robust smoky black tea is produced when the leaves are fired over open pine fires. It is made from the larger souchong leaves of the plant, is perfect for hearty breakfasts and robust meals, and is preferred during the cold months. I am always surprised to discover how fond women are of this tea; because of its deep, rich smoky flavor I used to believe it was a "man's tea."

Pu'erh: This is an earthy, distinct-tasting black or green tea that may be aged buried in the ground or in caves, which provide it with its strong aroma and taste. For more on *pu'erh* tea, see page 28.

Keemun: This small-leafed tea is renowned for its orchid bouquet and splendid red color. It is a sweet, mild black tea that is the perfect accompaniment to most meals and makes a splendid evening sip. This has been called the true "ambassador of teas" because it is so universally enjoyed. I am fond of this tea—it is like an old friend who is all the more admired because of his familiarity. Keemun tea was the tea used for the first English Breakfast teas, and interesting to note, one of two teas that age well.

Yunnan: This black tea is pleasantly robust with a chocolatey aftertaste, which has earned it its moniker, "the mocha of tea." It is grown in Yunnan Province and has long been considered one of the finest varietals on the planet—in fact, it is among the oldest of teas, having been cultivated for at least seventeen hundred years. It is versatile and widely cherished the world over and is referred to as a noble tea. I also sometimes think of this as the grand old man of tea with just a little pomp and majesty and a touch of stuffiness. It is superb with breakfast or as an afternoon pick-me-up. Yunnan tea, unlike other Chinese teas, tolerates a drop of milk.

GREEN TEAS

Gunpowder: So called because the tea leaves are rolled by hand into tiny pellets that resemble gunpowder in appearance, this tea is grassy and fresh-tasting. The tea is best in the late afternoon with strong tasting foods, as it cleanses the palate very nicely. In Arab countries, Gunpowder teas typically are mixed with mint for those countries' famed mint teas. Gunpowder tea is a good choice for anyone (particularly restaurateurs) looking for a "fail-safe" green tea that complements numerous dishes.

Temple of Heaven and Pin Head Tea: When Gunpowder tea is of especially fine quality, it is called one of these two names. The tea leaves are handrolled and unfurl into long, green banners. You can

Yixing Pots

These pots, which have been made in China for centuries, are clay pots that are particularly good for infusing tea. With each use, the pot seasons and adds to the fresh flavor of the tea.

Yixing pots are handcrafted from clay from the village of Dingshu in the province of Jiangsu. The soft yellow clay contains iron, quartz, and mica and when fired, turns a characteristic red color. However, blue and white clay is also found in the Yixing clay deposits and may be incorporated into the pots as well.

The clay is produced using an ancient and time-consuming method that insures a smooth, dense shell of clay. After it is dug, the clay is dried, pounded into powder, and then sifted through bamboo strainers to purify it. The fine powder is mixed with clear, cool water, and then, when its texture is correct, is left to dry naturally in the sun. It is then cut into blocks and sold to potters.

watch them unfurl when they are mixed with the boiling water. It is a mild, fresh tea with a clean palate and fine for drinking all day long.

Lung Ching (Dragon's Well): The best known and prized of Chinese green teas, Lung Ching is grown high in the Tieh Mu Mountains in Zhejiang Province; Dragon's Well is the village where the tea is produced. The green tea has a lovely aroma and extremely delicate flavor enhanced by sweet notes. It is perfect for serene occa-

The potters use heavy wooden mallets to pound the clay, mixing it with water as they do so, until it is of a workable viscosity—a process that takes about two days. The time-honored test to determine if the clay is ready is to slice it with a knife. The cut sides must be smooth and shiny without a trace of air pockets. Only then can it be shaped into pots.

Yixing pots are only one kind of pot used for making tea, but they are excellent. They are not designed for stovetop use, but when tea leaves and boiling water meet inside one of these vessels, the resulting beverage is gloriously refreshing. These pots are collectibles and increase in value not only with time but with use—evidenced by the patina on the outside of the pot and the flavor buildup on the inside.

sions and after large meals. It is what I consider an important tea, though often expensive.

OOLONG TEAS

Fenghuang Dancong: Chinese oolong teas are lighter and greener than Taiwanese oolongs, with a sharper, more astringent flavor and a green-gold color. This tea needs to be infused for only a minute or so before being enjoyed.

Ti Kuan Yin: This oolong is from Fujian Province and is a favorite among Chinese oolongs. The name translates as "iron goddess of mercy." The curled leaves produce a lovely, fragrant amber liquid that tastes tender and peachy on the palate. This tea needs three minutes of infusion.

Pi Lo Chun: This lovely tea requires very brief steeping in not-quite-boiling water to achieve its gorgeous color and expansive aroma. It is one of the rarest and finest of China's teas. It was the first tea that made me truly appreciate how different the same teas can taste depending on processing. The difference between Chinese Pi Lo Chun and Taiwanese Pi Lo Chun is marked—and both are intoxicating.

WHITE TEAS

Yin Zhen (Silver Needle): This tea allegedly is still produced by "imperial plucking," which means that the tea is harvested only two days a year and thus is greatly prized. This is no longer literally the case, but this fine tea is one of the world's most glamorous and expensive. When I hold a cup in my hands, I am tantalized by its gentle warmth and radiating but evasive aroma. Its light, fragrant palate commands my personal appreciation and respect.

Pai Mu Tan: This is a smooth and flowery tea with a hint of earthiness and is lovely to drink after a long day. It is picked during the early spring when the fine plucking is especially tender.

POUCHONG TEAS

Jasmine: Traditionally, jasmine petals are used to make a lightly scented tea. Scented teas differ from flavored teas in that the flower petals are tossed with the tea leaves thirteen times to infuse the leaves with their scent. Scented teas are typically made with lightly oxidized pouchong teas. A similar scented tea is made in Taiwan.

Rose: Similar to Jasmine but made with rose petals, rose-scented pouchong teas are among the world's most admired scented teas. Scented teas are meant to be drunk plain for a soothing effect. A similar scented tea is made in Taiwan.

India

The Indian subcontinent is home to numerous major tea-producing regions, notably Assam, Cachar, Darjeeling, Dehra Dun, Dooars, Kangra, Kerala, Manispur, Nilgiri, Terai, and Travancore. The most celebrated of these are Assam, Darjeeling, and to a lesser extent Nilgiri, with Dooars receiving honorable mention.

Tea production has expanded only since the English first made it a major crop in the early part of the nineteenth century. Today, the country ranks as one of the largest producers of tea in the world—if not the largest—with annual harvests exceeding 800,000 tons. Half of India's tea is produced in Assam alone. Indian tea growers are known for innovation and progressive ideas as well as for producing some of the finest teas the world knows. These teas were developed to appeal to Western tastes—which means they are almost universally black, or fermented, teas—but some Indian oolong, pouchong, and white teas are as subtle as any coming from China and Taiwan.

BLACK TEAS

Assam (region): Assam is the original Indian tea and is grown in northeast India, which is the largest tea-producing region in the world. It is a hearty, malty tea that is the traditional breakfast tea and as such can stand up to milk. Assam is the base for standard blends such as Irish and English Breakfast teas. I think of this as a powerful tea that lifts and pleases as few teas do. If Chinese teas are reflective, Indian teas are athletic. The fullness of a great, mellow, golden tippy Assam is immeasurably pleasurable.

Kondoli Organic GFOP: This is a lovely tea with lots of buds that infuses into a red-colored beverage with full, robust body and flavor. It is superb as a morning tea with a hearty English breakfast of eggs and sausage or later in the day with high tea, a simple meal sometimes called meat tea.

Darjeeling (region): Grown in the foothills of the Himalayas at altitudes of six thousand feet, Darjeeling tea is one of the most famous in the world and considered by many to be the best, which is why it is referred to as the Champagne of teas. It has a nutty note, pronounced greenness, strong character, and a gentle disposition, ready to satisfy any time of the day or the year. Top Darjeeling teas command high prices, in part because of their superior quality and in part because their season is limited to the months between March and September. The first flush of tea is picked after the spring rains arrive in March and April, the second flush in May and June, and then the final, autumnal harvest in September.

Darjeeling is the serendipitous result of an early attempt by the English to grow the Chinese *jat*, or tea plant, in the Assam region. Chinese *jat* weather the cold extremely well and so are often found at high elevations. The eventual hybrid of Chinese and Assam tea plants became one plant in the triumvirate that is now the source of excellent Darjeeling tea.

My days are not complete without Darjeeling tea. When I sip the first cup in the morning, every sense awakens and the mature bouquet reminds me not to take anything for granted. It is said that the finer a Darjeeling is, the harder it is to describe; this quality only increases my admiration.

Castleton SFTGOP First Flush: This is a popular Darjeeling with a superb aroma, sharp green notes, and a muscatel flavor that combines with an entrancing aftertaste. This is an excellent afternoon tea to be served with savory tea sandwiches.

Margaret's Hope FTGFOP: This aromatic, sweet tea made on a Darjeeling estate is noted for its subtle flavor and smooth palate and is a very good choice indeed to serve with a classic afternoon tea service.

Makaibari FTGOP1S: (Bio Dynamic) My personal favorite, this tea combines strong character and a delicate nutty disposition and as such makes a very good breakfast tea. Its nutty notes also make it delicious with Indian samosas, pakoras, or potato vadas at lunchtime.

Makaibari Oolong: This tea is produced with an alternate processing technique to make a unique cup that is unmistakably Darjeeling. The light roundness of the oolong, which is not as fully fermented as black teas, is evidenced by the tea's fresh palate, a Darjeeling trademark. This is a tea to savor on its own.

What Does a Teaman Drink?

I drink tea all day long as a necessity of life and as a function of my occupation. Just the act of preparing the tea is a ceremony of sorts and serves to ground me as I go about the daily business of living.

The most important of these everyday tea ceremonies is breakfast. Setting the right tone in the morning helps me get through the rest of the day. I am more than content with a freshly toasted bagel spread with butter and a pot of Darjeeling. I may choose to have eggs or palacinka *(thin, crepelike Croatian pancakes), but I never vary the tea. Breakfast may be over in thirty minutes or less, but putting the water on to boil, measuring the tea, and then steeping it are all vital to my well-being, making my precious Darjeeling integral to my rising ceremony.*

As the day progresses, I choose different teas depending on my activity. Gardening and more strenous exercise call for robust

Namring Upper SFGFOP1 Second Flush: A tea with a strong, defined character with hints of the greenness of the first flush, this is a great sipping tea with afternoon sweets.

Dooar (region): A strong, full-bodied tea, this tea, grown at relatively low altitudes, nevertheless is milder than Assam. Like Assam, it stands up to a little milk any time during the day.

Nilgiri (region): The Nilgiris, or Blue Mountains, spread across the southwestern tip of India at an altitude of forty-five hundred feet. Nilgiri teas are often used in blends, although the region is

Assams and Ceylons. More cerebral activities lend themselves to green and oolong teas, usually served in single-serving pots or covered cups.

In the evening, I turn to greens, pouchongs, and oolongs with the occasional silver tip Darjeeling or white tea. These help me focus as I write or study. While working late into the night, I find myself pondering over the tea, gazing into the liquor in the white cup. I watch the steam rising from the surface of the tea and note the color and depth of the tea. If I am stuck on a point, I find that one of the best ways to sort out my mind is to sit by the kettle and listen to the different tonalities of the water as it comes to the boil. Although I could almost imitate these sounds, so often have I listened to them, I find that the slow climax of heat and water clears my thought process.

moving into producing finer single-estate teas, too. I can't help but think of Nilgiri teas as "little brothers" who will never be able to measure up to the big boys, but will not stop trying.

Tigerhill OP: The long, beautiful black tea leaves brew into a brisk, clear tea that is best taken as an afternoon tea with sandwiches and simple pastries.

Terai (region): Grown to the south of Darjeeling. This tea is spicy and deeply hued. The tea can be drunk all day and is often found in blended teas.

Travancore (region): For a morning tea that combines the best of Darjeeling-style and Ceylon-style teas, this dark red, full-flavored tea is great in the morning and tolerates a little cold milk very nicely.

Taiwan

The island of Taiwan used to be known as Formosa, which explains why the teas produced there are also referred to as Formosa oolong teas. Tea has been cultivated and processed at relatively low altitudes on the island for three hundred years and nearly all of it becomes oolong tea. Oolong tea is fermented, as is black tea, but the fermentation is shorter in duration, yielding a tea that is 15 to 75 percent fermented. Most Chinese oolongs are only 15 percent fermented, while Formosa oolongs are often 75 percent fermented. Nowadays, the Taiwanese are making lighter oolongs that are fermented as little as 15 percent or even less called Jade oolong and Amber oolong. Because of this relatively low fermentation percentage, these teas are actually pouchong teas.

OOLONG TEAS

Oolong: Taiwanese oolong tea has distinctive nutty notes intertwined with subtle peachiness. It is semioxidized, which means it is fermented only 15 to 75 percent. When the fermentation is below 15 percent, it is referred to as pouchong tea. Oolong is the tea of choice for Yixing pots and is said to bring luck the more often it is infused. Yixing pots are famous clay pots made in China. (For more on these pots, see page 38.)

Imperial Oolong: Amber-colored tea with a slight taste of honey, this oolong is considered to be among the best in the world. It is part of the Oriental Beauty or Black Dragon family of teas, best known as evening teas.

Formosa White Tip Oolong: This full-bodied tea is made from well-formed leaves with lots of tips, or buds, and should be washed briefly before infusing to release the fragrance. Most of the time the tea should be steeped for three minutes, although some drinkers prefer the tea steeped a little longer. This is an excellent dessert tea—especially good with chocolate and crème brûlée.

Tung Ting: This is one of the most famous teas produced in Taiwan, with a mild flavor and reddish color. It is meant to be served all day and into the evening.

POUCHONG TEAS

Formosa Grand Pouchong: A lightly oxidized tea, this pouchong is close to being a green tea. When infused, it is pale yellow and has a light, mild flavor and distinctive aroma.

Jasmine: Traditionally, jasmine petals are used to make a lightly scented tea. These differ from flavored teas in that the flower petals are tossed with the tea leaves thirteen times to infuse the leaves with their scent. Scented teas typically are made with lightly oxidized pouchong teas.

Rose: Similar to Jasmine but made with rose petals, rose-scented pouchong teas are among the world's most admired scented teas. Scented teas are meant to be drunk plain for a soothing effect.

Sri Lanka

The climate and topography of this island nation are ideal for growing tea, which is by far its largest agricultural crop. When the nation, long called Ceylon in the West, gained its independence in 1972, it renamed itself Sri Lanka. However, the tea produced in estates in the verdant hills is still called Ceylon. Sri Lanka was once the world's largest exporter of tea, but economic and political setbacks have forced it to drop a few notches in this category. Nevertheless, it remains a top producer and certainly an esteemed one, being known for some of the best tea estates in the world. Until the 1860s, the island's primary crop was coffee, but the coffee plants were obliterated by the fungus *Hemileia vastatrix.* The coffee drinkers' loss was the tea drinkers' gain. Ceylon teas fall as neatly as any into the grading system, as I mention in the descriptions following. They also are able to stand up to the addition of cold milk, which has made them popular with generations of English tea lovers.

BLACK TEAS

Ceylon: This black tea is very flavorful and mildly astringent, with enough body to stand up to milk. Its beautiful long, thin leaves steep to make a mellow tea that is a favorite the world over.

Allen Valley: Known as an excellent FOP tea (Flowery Orange Pekoe), this tea is made from high-quality fine-plucked leaves with golden buds that give it a mellow flavor. This is an afternoon tea of distinction.

Berubeula: Here is another FOP of distinction that makes a delightful afternoon tea.

Nuwara Eliya: This rich, heady, brisk OP (Orange Pekoe) tea is produced at high altitudes. It is a tea with a lovely bouquet and excellent clarity that sometimes is referred to as the Champagne of Ceylon teas, one of my favorites.

Kenilworth: The long leaves produce bright red color and a robust aroma in a tea that is brisk and strong. This tea accommodates milk very nicely and is best enjoyed in the mid- to late afternoon.

Nature's Garden (or Koslande) Organic: This estate produces a smooth OP black tea that is delicious served with traditional afternoon tea fare. This is also a favorite, and a strong recommendation.

Pettigalla: Similar to the teas produced by the Kenilworth estate, the slightly fruity OP tea grown and processed on this estate is wonderful as an afternoon tea.

Dyraaba: This FP (Flowery Pekoe) tea is a well-balanced, aromatic one that serves as a morning or afternoon tea.

Uva Highlands: As another example of an FP tea that can be served morning or afternoon, this is a full-flavored brew. Also from this estate is a superior BOP (Broken Orange Pekoe) tea that is wonderful in the morning.

Saint James: From this estate comes an excellent BOP with good character and full flavor, two qualities of a good morning beverage.

Cupping: The Teaman's Task

In order to cup tea, which is to evaluate it, the teaman must have a "laboratory." This need not be a sleek, twenty-first-century high-tech work station, but should be a clean, light, and airy space, equipped with running water, a stove, a large work table, and storage areas. The laboratory, or cupping room, should be free of odors. It should be quiet, away from distractions such as television, the radio, the telephone, and any area where people are coming and going.

Cupping is the process we go through to judge the value of a tea and is a teaman's most important task. Because our bodies go through a series of chemical changes during the day, it is advisable to cup at the same time every day, in the same environment, and with conditions from one day to the next as consistent as possible.

Cupping essentials are usually made up of a kettle, a pot, a bowl, a teaspoon, and a scale. There should also be a spittoon or sink to spit into. The tea leaves are infused in the pot, which resembles a cup with a lid. At one side of the cup are serrated teeth, which trap the tea leaves when the infused tea is poured from the cup.

Most of the time I test six teas at once, lining them up behind six cupping pots. It's a good idea to compare apples with apples, which means I taste six oolongs or six Ceylon teas at once, rather than trying to compare pouchongs with black teas, for example.

To begin, I weigh two grams of tea for each pot. When the water boils, I pour a reasonable amount into each pot, making sure to add the same amount to each. As I pour, I watch the reaction of the leaves to the water—a process that is aptly called "the agony of the leaves."

Once the infusion has steeped for the appropriate amount of time, I place the pot in its bowl and tip the pot so that the tea flows over the serrated teeth into the bowl, but the leaves stay in the pot. Next I lift the pot to my nose and savor the aroma of the hot, wet leaves before tipping them into the pot's lid for examination. I use the teaspoon to taste or "cup" the tea, slurping the liquor off the spoon with a loud slurp so that the tea is sprayed all over the mouth. This ensures that every part of the tongue and throat taste the tea at the same time. I play (aerate) the tea in my mouth to determine its astringency before I spit it out and cup the next tea.

When cupping teas I judge the dry leaf on appearance and feel; the wet leaf on aroma and color; and the tea liquor on color, aroma, and flavor. I take copious notes on each and rank each characteristic from one to five. A tea that achieves a score of thirty is brilliant; one that gets only six points is relegated to the garden mulch pile.

GREEN TEAS

Ceylon: Green Ceylon tea is a rarity, but well worth drinking when found. It is marvelously aromatic and mellow with the subtle character and full body of the black Ceylon tea.

Nature's Garden OP (or Koslande): Most teas produced in Sri Lanka are black teas, but this estate makes a fresh, fruity green tea as well as a black tea. The green tea marries well with the flavors of fresh greens or roasted vegetables and so is a pleasant accompaniment to a lunch or a light supper. It is a serendipitea favorite.

Japan

Most of the tea grown in Japan is consumed in Japan, which is a shame, since some of the best green tea in the world is cultivated here. Japanese tea estates yield a little more than 110,000 tons of tea annually from about 148,000 acres, which is not a particularly large crop. The tea estates, which are in the south of the island, are carefully laid out, with long, evenly spaced rows of hedgelike tea plants extending across the fields. The Japanese drink predominately green tea—tea that is withered but never oxidized and which, when infused, is pale with a yellow or green tint. It is recognized for its digestive capabilities as well as its flavor and soothing aroma.

GREEN TEAS

Sencha: A true gem, this green tea is fresh, grassy, refreshing, and cooling—a perfect Japanese tea. When made, Sencha tea may be bright green or lighter, with the higher quality teas infusing greener and tasting more vegetal than the lesser teas, which are paler and grassier. All green teas have a comforting aroma.

Sencha Honyama: This is one of the teas that has made Japan famous for green teas. It is pale green in color and is blessed with a clean, flowery flavor that makes it especially relaxing and soothing.

Bancha: Although very good, Bancha teas are the poorer grades of Sencha teas, characterized by irregular leaves. The grassy-tasting, light amber liquid is served with simple foods such as noodles and sushi.

Bancha Houjicha: This green tea is crisp and nutty-tasting because the leaves are roasted. Unlike other green teas, the infused liquid appears light brown in color. It is a perfect accompaniment to meals.

Gyokuro: The Gyokuro tea plant produces what is considered to be the best leaf teas in Japan. The plants are kept shaded for the first three weeks of May to encourage a high chlorophyll content, low tannin, and a leaf with a dark emerald-green color that, when processed, is very fine, almost to the point of being powdery. The tea when steeped is served alongside raw or lightly seared fish and seafood and has earned the reputation for being a tea to serve those with a secure place in your heart. Gyokuro tea is also known as "pearl dew" tea.

Matcha Uji: This very special tea is made for a tea ceremony called *Cha-no-yu*. The tea itself is made from the leaves of the Gyokuro tea plant, and the brewing method is an ancient one that was adopted by the Japanese from China's Song Dynasty. Water is heated just until steam rises from the surface. The powdered tea is sprinkled over the water and the infusion is whisked until it froths and turns a brilliant jade green. The flavor of this unusual tea is reminiscent of fresh seaweed and is generally considered an acquired taste.

Genmaicha: To some, this may seem a novelty tea. It is made from mixing green tea with roasted rice and popcorn, the result of a tea shortage during World War II, and is now a favorite Japanese treat.

FLAVORED GREEN TEAS

Passion Fruit Sencha: Drinking this tea is a great way to end the day and spend the evening, as it combines the freshness of Sencha with the sweetness and fullness of passion fruit.

Tea Blends and Flavored Teas

During the heyday of the tea trade, the Chinese and the English tea merchants in India added flavors and fragrances to teas to expand their marketability to a wide range of taste preferences. Cinnamon, citrus, oil of bergamot, and cardamom were only some of the flavorings used to enhance the appeal of the less-than-top-quality teas. Tea leaves also were blended to produce what became popular blends, such as English Breakfast and Irish Breakfast teas.

Often, by combining two or more different leaves that complement each other but on their own are not particularly good, a tea is created with a whole far greater than its parts. When tea experts blend tea or taste blended teas, they must rely on their mental library of tea profiles to sort through the teas either to create a blend worth drinking or to distinguish which leaves are used. It is easy to understand that blending is a science with a dusting of art and one that requires focused skills and aptitudes. Following are some of the best known blends and flavored teas. When flowers or fruits are combined with tea leaves for flavored teas they are not blends. Lapsang Souchong is not a blend; its distinct flavor is achieved by its processing.

BLENDS

English Breakfast: A blending of small-leafed BOP Ceylon tea and teas from Keemun, although now it is just as often a blending of Assam or Darjeeling or other teas. This is a classic English morning tea that stands up well to milk and is served with typical Western breakfast fare.

Irish Breakfast: Similar to English Breakfast, this blend is hearty and full-flavored. Traditionally it has been a blend of strong Assam tea leaves and Ceylon tea.

Five O'Clock Tea: As the name implies, this tea blended from Ceylon teas is meant to be drunk in the afternoon as an accompaniment to sweets and pastries. Many tea drinkers add milk to this tea, but aficionados generally do not.

SCENTED CHINESE BLACK TEAS

Earl Grey: One of many legends claims that Earl Grey, scented with the oil of bergamot, was developed by the Chinese for Britain's envoy to China Earl Grey in 1830. Oil of bergamot is made from a Cantonese citrus fruit and gives this world-favorite a bright, spicy flavor. As popular as Earl Grey tea is with the rest of the world, the Chinese are not known for drinking it.

Tisanes

Just as the Latin Camellia sinensis *refers to the tea we discuss in this book, the Latin* Anthemis nobilis *or* Chamaemelum nobile *refers to chamomile, and the Latin* mentha *and* lavandula *refer to mint and lavender. But there is greater meaning to the word* tea *beyond being the beverage infused from the Camellia* sinensis *plant's leaves. It often is tossed about when* any hot *drink made from boiling water and edible leaves is meant.*

I am fond of such beverages but, on purist grounds, object to the term herb tea. *These are tisanes and should be identified by the term* tisane.

Tisanes are favorites with those who eschew caffeine and therefore do not indulge in the beverage I call tea. They are often taken after a large evening meal to soothe digestion and encourage slumber. They may also be drunk for medicinal purposes.

Both large and small tea companies market tisanes, hoping to capture a segment of the population otherwise untouched by the lure of tea. In recent years, these infusions have earned a reputation for being "healthier" and more wholesome than either tea or coffee and, as such, have been given poetic names. In reality, these are simple infusions that satisfy the taste buds, theoretically soothe some ills, and are generally harmless sips.

Chamomile, made from chamomile flowers, has a smooth floral flavor and calming properties. It is commonly drunk by those seeking sleep or relaxation. Used as a poultice, chamomile tea is said to fight acne and eczema and to ease strain.

Lemon balm tisanes are said to relieve depression and soothe stomach upset. The fresh leaves, applied directly to the skin, bring relief from insect bites. The same is said of mint leaves, which, when steeped in boiling water, become a tisane known to relieve indigestion and sweeten the breath.

Lavender, when brewed as a tisane, is claimed to soothe and relax the spirit; elderberry and elderflower tisanes to help migraine, relieve sore throat, induce sleep, and be calming. Rose-hip tisane, one of the favorites and rich in vitamin C, is credited with soothing coughs while stimulating mental activity. Hibiscus tisane is another good source of vitamin C and its potent fruity flavor is a wake-up call to anyone who has indulged in too much chamomile.

Tisanes can be custom-blended and infused in your own kitchen, with any edible herb leaf, either fresh or dried. With dried leaves, use about a tablespoon of gently torn leaves for every two cups of water; with fresh, increase the amount of herb to two table-spoons. Pour the boiling water over the leaves and let the tisane infuse for three to five minutes. These instructions and amounts are meant only as guides; use your own judgment and taste to create tisanes. Many people add lemon or honey or both to tisanes.

Imperial Russian: This tea is close to Earl Grey in flavor, being scented with the oil of bergamot, too, but it is fruitier. Originally made in China, the tea caught the fancy of Russian nobility in the nineteenth century, hence the name.

serendipitea's Liliuokalani: This falls under the heading of a tropical China black tea because of its tropical lushness and richness of color. It tastes of peaches, mangoes, apples, oranges, and guavas. It is a relatively new entry into the world of tea, being named after the last queen of Hawaii.

serendipitea's Twilight: Soft chamomile and gentle lavender flavor this black tea for a full-bodied tea that is as relaxing as it is tasty.

serendipitea's Black Velvet: This unusual combination of ginseng, peppermint, and licorice flavoring black Chinese tea is considered recuperative and relaxing.

Orchid: Seductively exotic, orchid tea is soft and mellow with a lovely fragrance, and yet is distinct and strong at the same time.

Magnolia: This newcomer to the flavored black tea category is perfumed with the gracious and aromatic flower of the American South.

Cassis: The flavor of black currants mingling with the Chinese Anhui Province black tea does nothing but enhance this elegant and refined tea. This exemplifies what flavored teas are meant to be: uncluttered and good.

SCENTED CHINESE GREEN TEA

serendipitea's Rose Alongi: This soft, rose-scented tea is a gentle flavored tea in the best tradition of scented teas.

Jasmine Yin Hao: This is a traditional scented tea with a melodic coupling of fragrant sweet petals and light, slightly sweet green tea.

Other Tea-Producing Countries

While the five countries previously listed produce the jewels of the crown, other countries contribute handsomely to the wealth of the global tea market. Most of the tea-producing countries other than those already discussed make black tea, which is the preferred type throughout Europe and the Americas, as well as much of India, Pakistan, the Arab countries, and Africa. To grasp the breadth of the tea business, it is necessary only to glance at tea production in the rest of the world.

Vietnam: At the dawn of the nineteenth century, the French established tea estates in Vietnam, which never produced great quantities of tea, so that by the following century, they went into decline. Since the end of the Vietnam War, the tea estates have been revitalized and the country's tea industry is greatly admired for its rapid development and fine teas. Today, a soft green tea called Ha Giang is a popular Vietnamese tea. With its undertones of fruit and hints of grass, the tea has been grown and consumed for centuries in Vietnam, although it is still little known elsewhere. This is a wonderful accompaniment to fruit-based desserts.

Nepal: Considering the altitude of the country, it is not surprising that these teas are reminiscent of those from Darjeeling. They are full-bodied teas meant to be drunk in the afternoon without milk.

Bangladesh: The black teas from Bangladesh are dark, spicy, and pleasingly aromatic. Consumed all day long, they taste good with milk or without.

Indonesia: Not surprisingly, teas from this part of the world resemble those from Sri Lanka: full-bodied black teas that are delicious in the morning.

Argentina: Teas produced here taste earthy and steep to a dark red. They are typical morning-style teas that are good with or without milk.

Malaysia: The BOP teas from Malaysia are establishing a reputation as flavorful morning teas that stand up to milk.

Russia: The teas grown in Georgia are pleasant, full-bodied teas with flowery overtones that are acceptable afternoon and evening teas. When the tea leaves are broken (BOP), they infuse into a typical breakfast tea. Unhappily, since the fall of the Soviet Union, Georgian tea estates have all but disappeared. We can hope they will be revitalized.

Kenya: Teas from this East African nation bear watching as they resemble the best of Assam teas. Their flavor is full and fruity and, when steeped, they are golden-hued.

Cameroon: Grown at relatively high altitudes, these teas are flavorful and fare well on the world market. They can be drunk with or without milk.

Turkey: Turkish teas are more closely akin to Chinese teas than to Indian teas. They are slightly sweet and are meant to be drunk unadorned in the late afternoon and evening.

Teatime

In every part of the globe, the simple, everyday act of making and drinking tea has customs attached to it. At their very core, these customs speak to the human need for community and shared experience. Just as when I was growing up in Australia and my mother offered tea to our neighbors and fellow Croatian immigrants as a gesture of hospitality, and just as the young student in sixth-century B.C. China reportedly offered a bowl of tea to the traveling Taoist philosopher, Lao-tzu, tea arguably is the most basic universal symbol of hospitality.

Tea also can be a solitary drink. A steaming cup is a familiar accompaniment to an engrossing novel. We pour tea on damp afternoons, holding the cup with both hands as we gaze at the rain pattering on the pavement. From ancient days, tea and deep contemplation have gone hand in hand, a fact documented centuries ago by the Chinese, who insisted that tea enhanced mental clarity.

Throughout England, Ireland, Wales, Scotland, Bermuda, Canada, Australia, New Zealand, and other countries included in the far-flung borders of the Commonwealth, tea shops and tearooms are familiar. Just as commonplace are elegant afternoon teas served in hotel lobbies and on landscaped terraces. In homes across these nations, tea kettles whistle around the four o'clock hour, signaling the moment when life slows down for a short while, when we can relax, enjoy the tea, and perhaps a biscuit or slice of cake.

In Japan, tea is served with great ceremony involving a special tea-room and the host's honoring his guests by following ancient customs and using specified utensils and dishes. In other countries, too, prescribed customs surround tea-taking. In Myanmar, men gather daily at tea stands to discuss the events of the day, argue, reminisce, and, yes, drink tea. Indians on the subcontinent drink "cha-ya" or street tea all day long, stopping frequently to buy a cup of the milky beverage. In Morocco and other North African countries, sweet mint tea, strong enough to challenge the most hardened coffee drinker, is poured into small glass cups at shops, in bazaars, and at sidewalk cafés. No business transaction is considered before a cup of tea is consumed by all involved parties.

In America, tea is often served iced. In the southern part of the country, pitchers of highly sweetened iced tea are placed on tables at roadhouses, barbecue pits, and church suppers. Although Americans rely on tea bags far more than loose-leaf tea for the beverage, they are learning to use loose tea, as evidenced by the rise in small tea shops and elegant emporiums, which are opening around the nation.

Steeping the Perfect Cup of Tea

Begin by bringing fresh, cool water to a boil in a kettle. Use the water you like best, but if your tap water tastes of chemicals, use spring water. Warm the teapot with hot water. Discard the water and then spoon the tea leaves into the pot. Allow one level teaspoon for each cup. The heat of the pot will release the bouquet of the leaves. When the water boils, immediately remove the kettle from the stove and pour the water over the leaves. It is important to bring the tea to the kettle, not the kettle to the tea. This ensures that the water will be hot enough. Let the tea steep for as long as the particular kind of tea requires. Vary the time according to personal taste, but keep in mind that steeping any tea for longer than five minutes does not contribute to flavor, only to bitterness.

Steeping times

WHITE TEA: *30 seconds to 2 minutes*

GREEN TEA: *1 to 3 minutes*

POUCHONG: *1 to 3 minutes*

GREEN OOLONG TEA: *2 to 3 minutes*

BLACK OOLONG TEA: *up to 5 minutes*

BLACK TEA: *up to 5 minutes (except Darjeeling, which should be steeped for 3 or 4 minutes)*

For most Westerners, teatime means British teatime: Wedgwood china, a silver tea service, small plates piled with crustless sandwiches, and others filled with thin slices of lemon cake, steaming hot scones, homemade strawberry jam, and please don't forget the Devonshire cream! For many, this is the stuff of lovely fantasy.

Afternoon tea is a mainstay of British culture. When non-Britons think of English culture, they are as apt to conjure up an image of tea and crumpets as of the Globe Theatre or the royal family. Of course, it is in part due to the English aristocracy that tea is such a passion in the United Kingdom—first because of Anna, Duchess of Bedford, and then, later in the same century, because of Queen Victoria's appreciation for the afternoon meal.

When the duchess was in her prime in the early days of the nineteenth century, the aristocracy typically ate only two meals a day: a large and late breakfast and then a late-evening dinner. By the middle of the afternoon, the duchess was hungry, experiencing what she called "a sinking feeling." To ward off the pangs, she asked her staff to bring her a bracing cup of tea and a small sweet. Soon she was inviting friends to join her in the afternoon repast, and taking tea, complete with sweets and delicate sandwiches, quickly became fashionable.

The custom filtered down to the working classes, who no doubt embraced the afternoon tea ritual as a way to affirm a sense of community. Such a sense was eroding during the century when the nation's population moved from small villages to larger cities, responding to England's dramatic and impressive Industrial Revolution, which transformed the country into the most industrialized nation on earth.

This is not to say that the English had not been drinking tea for more than a century. Chests of Chinese tea arrived in London in 1644 for the first time, and their contents were immediately consumed. By 1700, more than five hundred coffeehouses in London offered "China Tcha, Tay, or Tee." Tea began a slow gain on ale as the breakfast beverage of choice among Englishmen. However, tea was still precious and would not be widely and conveniently available to all Britons until the middle of the following century. It was still very much a drink that was enjoyed in the private homes of the upper class.

Queen Victoria, who reigned from 1837 until 1901, loved afternoon tea. During her many years on the throne, she rarely missed it, whether she was in residence at Buckingham Palace or elsewhere. She introduced the habit of taking a slice of lemon with her tea, a custom she learned when visiting her eldest daughter, who was married to a Russian nobleman. Sponge cake reportedly was the queen's favorite sweet, served with a generous layer of strawberry jam and thick cream. But other sweets became familiar tea table treats, too—English culinary treasures such as Eccles cakes, lemon curd tarts, and apple turnovers.

Tea gardens opened throughout the country, catering to weekend and evening activities during the warm months of the year. Soon, the patrons of tea gardens found that light-hearted dancing was a good way to while away the tea hour, particularly if the activity was carried out in a subdued and civilized manner. This became the custom known as the tea dance, which was a fixture of British culture until World War II.

Tea Bags or Loose-Leaf Tea?

I have very little patience with tea bags and highly recommend that anyone who enjoys good tea learn how to steep it from loose leaves. It takes a little longer and may be slightly less convenient, but when it comes to good taste and full flavor, tea bags are a distant second to loose tea.

Why? you ask. When I speak about tea at seminars and other gatherings, I often use the analogy of a journey through beautiful scenery to explain my preference. You can choose to ride a horse through the verdant countryside, breathing in the fragrant air, reveling in the breathtaking vistas along the way. Or, you can choose to ride the train and read the paper, rarely glancing out the window as you zip down the tracks. Either choice will get you to the same destination—but you have to decide which is more to your liking.

Tea bags are terrific marketing tools and in America certainly are preferred to loose teas. The handy little sacks usually hold inferior tea, either tea leaf dust or fannings, which results in weak, rather bland-tasting tea. Higher-priced tea bags are stuffed with better leaves, often broken so that they infuse quickly in the boiling water, turning it deep red and quite flavorful. But these leaves are never as fine as those used for quality loose-leaf teas.

It's not unusual for CTC leaves to be used for tea bags. These are leaves that have been through a machine that "crushes, tears, and curls" the leaves to improve the qualities of what are otherwise very ordinary tea leaves. The process releases essential liquids in the leaves, making them therefore more flavorful than they otherwise might be. But is this a good reason to use tea bags? Why not go for the quality rather than the compromise?

Tea bags also infuse more quickly than leaf teas. To my mind this is their sole advantage. Infusion time may be a minute or less, while for loose-leaf tea infusion may be five minutes. I suppose in our fast-paced, hectic world this is an advantage, but drinking good tea should be relaxing and refreshing and generally worth five minutes of preparation.

The reason tea bags infuse more quickly than leaf tea is that they have greater surface area. Surface area as it relates to tea is defined by the standard of a hypothetical brick of tea leaves with a total surface area of forty square inches. If you break the brick in half, the surface area increases to forty-eight square inches per half brick. If these are halved, the surface area of each is now sixty-four square inches, and so on until the brick is broken to dust and the surface area is one that I choose not to calculate. However, every time a new surface area is created, the infusion time decreases. Increased surface area also means more chance for bitterness, which is why it is prudent to keep a watchful eye on steeping tea bags. However, since they rarely are made with potent tea, this is not as much of an issue as it might be.

Because it was usually only the upper classes who could afford a substantial amount of time off for tea at four or five o'clock, the lower classes gradually adopted the custom of high tea or meat tea. This far simpler, yet more substantial meal, usually eaten in the kitchen instead of the drawing room, served as supper for most working-class families and was eaten at a table, like any other meal. The height of the table may explain the name: Tea was served on a high table as opposed to the low style of table that might be found in a more formal setting. It's interesting to note that this term is often misused in modern times, with people wrongly calling afternoon tea "high tea" in an attempt to sound sophisticated.

The British, whether inhabitants of the island nation or residing in another country, are known for preferring tea to all other beverages. While this is not universally true of Englishmen—some happily drink coffee or beer and leave tea to their friends—I think the English love tea because it is the essence of the English spirit. Here is a drink suitable for all, poor, rich, young, and old, that stimulates without requiring one to forfeit composure, or as poet William Cowper wrote, " . . . the cups that cheer but not inebriate."

THE CHARM OF AN ENGLISH AFTERNOON TEA

Depending on their station, Queen Victoria's subjects indulged in afternoon tea or high tea, consuming copious amounts of the beverage and creating an ever-expanding set of rules and rituals to accompany it. The queen may not have intended to initiate a social revolution, but she succeeded nonetheless. Today, the average Briton drinks six cups of tea a day. The Victorian custom of late-afternoon calling among the

Teacups and Saucers

When tea first became fashionable in Britain in the mid-seventeenth century, Catherine of Braganza, the Portuguese princess who married Charles II, established it as the beverage at court. Her contemporary, the Duchess of York, introduced the custom to Scotland where, it is believed, the Scots initiated the custom of pouring the hot tea into the saucer to facilitiate cooling. The habit, still in existence in some parts of the United Kingdom, could have survived into modern times as a misinterpretation of how to use the Chinese guywan—a lidded, handleless cup that nestles into a deep saucer so that it can be held without scalding one's fingers.

members of the upper classes effortlessly segued into elaborate and stylish tea parties; tea dances became formalized affairs; and elegant hotels and transatlantic steamships offered opulent teas in the late afternoon. In the summer, tea was taken in the gardens of large country estates, with servants frequently being asked to cart heavy tables and chairs to the most bucolic and remote areas of the private parks. In England today, tea served in the garden is considered a weekend treat.

The tea poured from English teapots was—and still is—black tea. Darjeeling, Assam, and Ceylon teas, which infuse into stimulating beverages with rich, red color or, in the case of Ceylon, golden hues, were the most commonly served teas. Later, Earl Grey and Five O'Clock blends became great favorites, as these comprised of the best teas of India and Ceylon (now Sri Lanka) while appealing to the palate's quest for new flavors.

English hostesses were proud of their acumen in steeping tea at the tea table. The water was kept hot in large silver urns and the lady of the house measured the tea directly from her ornate or antique tea caddy—a small chest for storing tea—into a heated porcelain pot. When it had steeped for the precise length of time, she poured the tea into thin, almost transparent cups, using a tea strainer to catch the leaves. She passed the cups to her guests, first quietly asking if they preferred milk or lemon, one lump or two. If they asked for milk, she poured it into the cup before the tea, an old custom about which many tea drinkers still feel passionate.

The ritual was serene and demure. Guests deferred to the hostess, following her lead in topics of conversation. Teatime was not for wicked gossip, political discussion, or rowdy conversation. It was the time for gentle news of family and friends, the weather, fashion, literature, and, if the group was quite avant-garde, the theater.

Today, an English afternoon tea is considered a treat indeed. Hotels in London, as well as some restaurants and upmarket stores such as Harrods, offer a chic late-day meal in lovely and sedate surroundings. Tea at the Ritz, the Savoy, the Dorchester, and the Connaught hotels is as desirable as it ever was, although because of its price, it is not an everyday occurrence for most people. In other cosmopolitan cities, too, afternoon tea is served in the English style, complete with delectable pastries and watercress and cucumber sandwiches made on tender white bread. At these meals the tea is steeped correctly (never made with tea bags) and poured into small, thin-shelled cups.

Cucumber and Smoked Salmon Tea Sandwiches with Dill Butter

MAKES 8 TRIANGULAR TEA SANDWICHES

½ cup (1 stick) unsalted butter, at room temperature

2 tablespoons chopped fresh dill

8 slices white bread, crusts trimmed

4 ounces sliced smoked salmon

⅓ English cucumber (about 4 inches), finely sliced (see Note)

In a small bowl, mix together the butter and dill, mashing gently with a fork until thoroughly blended.

Lightly spread the butter on one side of each slice of bread.

Lay slices of smoked salmon on 4 of the buttered bread slices, trimming the salmon to fit the bread. Layer the cucumber slices over the salmon and top with the remaining slices of bread. Cut each sandwich in half diagonally. Serve immediately or cover with a well-wrung damp kitchen towel until ready to serve.

Note: English cucumbers are longer than ordinary garden cucumbers and require no peeling. They have fewer seeds than other cucumbers, too. They often are sold wrapped in plastic.

Watercress and Chive Cream Cheese Tea Sandwiches

MAKES 8 TRIANGULAR TEA SANDWICHES

¼ cup cream cheese, at room temperature

1 tablespoon finely chopped fresh chives

8 slices white bread, crusts trimmed

1 small bunch fresh watercress, thick stems removed

In a small bowl, mix together the cream cheese and chives, mashing gently with a fork until thoroughly blended.

Lightly spread the cream cheese on one side of each slice of bread.

Lay sprigs of watercress on 4 of the bread slices and top with the remaining slices. Cut each sandwich in half diagonally. Serve immediately or cover with a well-wrung damp kitchen towel until ready to serve.

Radish and Dill Cream Cheese Tea Sandwiches

MAKES 8 TRIANGULAR TEA SANDWICHES

¼ cup cream cheese, at room temperature

1 tablespoon finely chopped fresh dill

8 slices white bread, crusts trimmed

4 to 6 red radishes, very thinly sliced

In a small bowl, mix together the cream cheese and dill, mashing gently with a fork until thoroughly blended.

Lightly spread the cream cheese on one side of each slice of bread.

Lay radish slices on 4 of the bread slices and top with the remaining slices. Cut each sandwich in half diagonally. Serve immediately or cover with a well-wrung damp kitchen towel until ready to serve.

Smoked Salmon and Jalapeño Cream Cheese Tea Sandwiches

MAKES 8 TRIANGULAR TEA SANDWICHES

¼ cup cream cheese, at room temperature

1 tablespoon finely minced jalapeño pepper

8 slices white bread, crusts trimmed

4 ounces sliced smoked salmon

Bean or broccoli sprouts

In a small bowl, mix together the cream cheese and jalapeño, mashing gently with a fork until thoroughly blended.

Lightly spread the cream cheese on one side of each slice of bread.

Lay slices of smoked salmon on 4 of the bread slices, trimming the salmon to fit the bread. Sprinkle some sprouts over the salmon and top with the remaining slices of bread. Cut each sandwich in half diagonally. Serve immediately or cover with a well-wrung damp kitchen towel until ready to serve.

Lemon Curd Tartlets

MAKES FOUR 4 1/2-INCH TARTLETS OR EIGHT 2 1/4-INCH TARTLETS

2 cups plus 3 tablespoons all-purpose flour

3/4 cup plus 2 tablespoons confectioners' sugar

9 tablespoons unsalted butter, cut into small pieces and well chilled

1 large egg

Unsalted butter, melted

One 11- or 12-ounce jar lemon curd (see Note)

Confectioners' sugar, for dusting

In a food processor, combine the flour and sugar and process until well mixed. Add the butter all at once and process until the mixture resembles coarse crumbs. Add the egg and process until the dough starts to hold together. Add ice water, a teaspoon at a time, if the dough is too dry. You should not need more than 3 teaspoons (1 tablespoon) of ice water.

Turn the dough out onto a clean, dry surface (not floured) and gather it into a disk. Wrap the disk in plastic wrap and refrigerate for at least 1 hour or overnight.

Unwrap the disk and divide it in half. Form one half into a smaller disk, wrap in plastic wrap, and freeze for another use. (It will keep for up to 1 month.)

Lightly brush four 4½-inch tartlet pans or eight 2¼-inch tartlet pans with melted butter. Arrange the pans so that they are sitting close together on the work surface.

On a lightly floured work surface, roll out the pastry dough so that it is about ⅛-inch thick. Carefully drape the dough over the tartlet pans and gently roll the rolling pin over it so that it is cut to the size of the tartlet pans. With a lightly floured thumb, gently press the pastry dough into the pans and up the sides. Trim any overhanging pastry. Prick the bottom of the dough with a fork and then refrigerate the lined tartlet pans for 1 hour.

Preheat the oven to 400°F.

Remove the tartlet pans from the refrigerator and line them with aluminum foil that is cut to be about 2 inches larger than the pans. Press the foil into the pans to conform to their shapes. Set the pans on a baking sheet and fill each one with dried beans, rice, or pie weights. Bake for 10 minutes. Remove from the oven and discard the foil and weights. Bake the shells for 5 to 10 minutes longer until the bottoms are dry and the pastry is golden. Cool on wire racks.

When completely cool, lift the pastry shells from the pans and fill each one with lemon curd. Dust with confectioners' sugar and serve.

Note: While you can make your own, commercially prepared lemon curd is very good. Buy it at specialty food stores.

Tea and Sweeteners

Although many people the world over sweeten tea, I do not. I like the fresh, pure flavor of tea, freshly and properly steeped. However, if you want to sweeten tea a little, I recommend pure white cane sugar and nothing else. The sugar may be loose or in cubes, but regardless of its form, take care not to add too much. I don't subscribe to the notion of tea and honey, except when speaking of tisanes—herbal infusions that seem to blend nicely with clover, orange blossom, or another kind of honey.

TEA AT OTHER TIMES IN ENGLAND

High tea, as explained, is as different from afternoon tea as an ice cream sundae is from a chocolate èclair. It is a workaday meal, served when the family arrives home from the office, school, or labor in the fields. Tea is only one element of the meal, which is actually the evening meal and may include cold meat, stew, soup, or a casserole. This is why it is sometimes referred to as meat tea.

Other English tea traditions include cream tea, nursery tea, elevenses, and ham tea. The first is a reference to England's magnificent Devonshire or clotted cream, also called Devon cream. It is made by heating rich, unpasteurized milk until the cream clots on top. When cooled, the super-thick cream is spooned off, denser and more delicious than whipped cream could ever be. At a traditional cream tea, the clotted cream is spread on freshly baked scones and then topped with straw-

English Tea Shops

As readers of Agatha Christie and Martha Grimes know, every high street in every village in Great Britain has a tea shop where the locals congregate during the day for a cup of tea and a light sandwich or slice of cake. But this was not always so. It was not until 1864 that the concept of the tea shop was born—surely an idea whose time had come. In that year, tea and simple baked goods were served by the innovative manager of the Aerated Bread Company in London as a way to increase walk-in trade. The idea was an overnight success, particularly with women who realized they had found a public venue for casual meetings that was not as scandalous as the local pub.

berry or raspberry preserves. It is not, as some uninitiated might think, added to the tea. Cream teas are afternoon treats.

A nursery tea is nothing more complicated than a tea prepared for children. In Victorian times, the children of the upper classes were relegated to their own suites of rooms under the supervision of nannies and tutors. Nursery teas were late-afternoon meals that the children and their caregivers enjoyed and were usually more simple than the elegant party taking place in the drawing room. Typically, the food served at nursery teas was the sort that children would enjoy—bread and honey, scones and jam, cinnamon toast, and perhaps milk or cider rather than actual tea. However, the English have never hesitated to let their children drink tea, unlike the French, who still frown on it.

Elevenses is a term referring to a late-morning snack of tea and a pastry. This simple pick-me-up is akin to the American coffee break and is a welcome spot in otherwise busy mornings in offices, factories, or private homes. Ham teas are small meals of tea and hearty sandwiches, instead of the dainty tea sandwiches associated with afternoon tea. Ham teas are notably popular in Scotland, where inclement weather makes robust fare appealing. At ham teas, refined etiquette takes a back seat to appetite, as guests are encouraged to assemble their own sandwiches.

Finally, let us not forget that welcome hot "cuppa" drunk first thing in the morning in bed, if you are fortunate enough to have it brought to you. Tea is the best accompaniment to a typical English breakfast of eggs, toast, and rashers (bacon), which to this day remains one of the Commonwealth's greatest gifts to the culinary world.

Tea in France

Although Paris and other French cities and towns are home to elegant *salons de thé*, the French are associated far more with the café scene where strong coffee and *vin ordinaire* are the order of the day. Despite this, the French imported tea a few years before the English did, although for decades after its introduction, it was considered mainly medicinal. During the later years of Louis XIV's reign (1643–1715), tea became a fashionable drink at court, just as it was in England, but unlike Englishmen, the ordinary Frenchman did not drink it until the end of the nineteenth century. During the

Playing the Irish Mother

It is better that one asks, "Shall I be Mother?" otherwise the host or hostess will ask "Who shall be Mother?" Among all the components of a good Irish tea, water, pot, tea leaves, milk, and sugar, the most important element is "Mother."

"Mother" is not the matron of the group, but anyone male, female, young or old, who accepts the responsibility of ensuring that the cups of the group are always filled. One person who is not "Mother" is the host or hostess, as this person will be too busy preparing and serving the refreshments and the food and welcoming the guests as they arrive.

intervening two hundred years or so, tea was the province of the aristocracy and intellectuals, enjoyed in private homes and select salons.

A much admired 1766 painting by French artist Olivier Barthélemy depicts the young Mozart playing the harpsichord while handsomely attired men and women take tea at marble-topped tables. The painting is called *Le Thé à l'Anglaise*, which is curious when you know that the French had been drinking tea as long as the English. This is only one example of tea playing a role in some of the art created at the time. In this and other instances tea is depicted as an accepted part of everyday life—among certain classes.

The Cups of Cronstadt

Although we know that teacups were made in China long before the Europeans began drinking tea, the first European-style cups were supposedly made in a German colony in Transylvania, Romania, called Cronstadt. The cups were made with a rendering of the city of Cronstadt painted on the bottom. When café proprietors skimped on tea leaves and made weak tea, customers would complain that they could "see Cronstadt" through the watery liquor. This was a happy situation for the tea drinkers, as they could easily catch a cheapskate in the act, but the café owners didn't like it at all. Cronstadt cups were phased out and replaced by tea glasses.

Tea played a role in other paintings by French artists (as well as those from other countries). A delightful 1742 painting by François Boucher called *Toilette* depicts two young women in the boudoir preparing to go out; teacups and a teapot are on a side table. The artist M. A. Baschet painted several generations enjoying tea around a table in a canvas called *Francisque Sarcey at the Home of Adolphe Brisson's Daughter.* All seem to be enjoying the party, including an obviously cherished child who has no tea within her grasp. The French never have approved of children drinking tea, because of its stimulant properties. Tea, too, was mentioned in works of Balzac, Racine, and, of course, Proust, who recalled drinking tea while eating madeleines.

Chocolate-Dipped Chocolate Madeleines

MAKES 24 MADELEINES

MADELEINES

2 tablespoons unsalted butter, melted

½ cup all-purpose flour, sifted

½ cup unsweetened Dutch-process cocoa

1 teaspoon baking powder

Pinch of salt

½ cup (1 stick) unsalted butter, at room temperature

½ cup granulated sugar

1 tablespoon pure vanilla extract

2 large eggs

4 large egg yolks

GANACHE

4 ounces bittersweet chocolate, finely chopped

½ cup heavy cream

1 tablespoon unsalted butter

1 tablespoon granulated sugar

To make the madeleines, preheat the oven to 375°F and position an oven rack in the center of the oven. Lightly brush 2 madeleine molds with the melted butter and dust the molds with flour. Tap out the excess flour.

In a bowl, sift together the flour, cocoa, baking powder, and salt. Set aside.

Using an electric mixer set on medium-high speed, cream the room-temperature butter until light and fluffy. Add the sugar and vanilla and mix well. Add the eggs and egg yolks and mix until smooth. Fold in the dry ingredients until blended. Spoon a heaping teaspoon of the batter into each mold. There is no need to smooth the batter; it will spread in the oven.

Arrange the molds side by side in the center of the oven and bake the madeleines for 10 to 12 minutes or until the madeleines spring back when pressed lightly. Invert the madeleines onto wire racks. Turn them so that the rounded, decorative sides face up. Cool completely on wire racks.

To prepare the ganache, put the chocolate in a stainless steel bowl.

In a saucepan, combine the cream, butter, and sugar and heat over medium-low heat until boiling. Stir to blend, let the hot cream sit for 40 to 60 seconds, and then pour over the chocolate. Stir until smooth and the chocolate melts. Let the ganache cool slightly; it should be quite warm and still liquid.

Dip the wide end of each cooled madeleine in the ganache and set aside on a parchment- or wax-paper–lined baking sheet in the refrigerator until the chocolate sets.

The French admired the fragile and exotically decorated teapots and cups brought to their shores by the tea traders from the Orient. They created fine china of their own design, inspired by these imports. With the interest in fine china came the custom of adding a little cold milk to hot tea. An aristocratic French woman named Madame de la Sablière allegedly introduced the idea to society because, she claimed, "it was to her taste." In fact, practical historians have observed that the cold milk prevented the hot tea from cracking the delicate porcelain, whether it was from China or made in France. This remains the accepted theory of why milk, when added to black tea, is poured into the cup first. The British insist on this custom to this day, even though as often as not tea is served in sturdy mugs and impervious modern-day china.

Not surprisingly, the French were serving exquisite pastries with tea well before the custom was as entrenched in England. Sleek *gateaux*, sweet *dacquoises*, and luscious fruit tarts were common on the French tea table, as were *pâte à choux* treats such as cream puffs and éclairs. To this day, French pastries are considered the pinnacle of teatime treats. Most people seeking a Western-style afternoon tea in sophisticated tearooms anywhere on earth are disappointed if these delicacies are not part of the menu.

With the lovely china and the elegant pastries, the French tea table has always been an appealing sight. It is generally more formal than an English tea table, although both share in the spirit of refined entertainment. Today, *salons de thé* thrive in Paris and throughout France, attracting young and more seasoned patrons alike with their attention to detail, good service, high-quality food, and excellent tea—all in an atmosphere probably not unlike the salons of the eighteenth and nineteenth centuries. Now as then, French tea drinkers are known for holding forth on the politics, literature, drama, music, and social customs of the day. Although the French may never match the English in terms of tea consumption, tea drinking is growing in France, spurred on by innovative marketing and the Frenchman's innate curiosity about new flavors and ways to enjoy food and drink.

Tea in Russia

Russians drink tea all day long, relying on the simmering samovar for "instant" hot water, which they use to dilute the strong green or black tea brewed in the teapot resting on top of the samovar. The warm, constantly bubbling samovar has long been at the center of Russian homelife, making rooms cozy and inviting. Writers from Tolstoy and Dostoyevsky to Chekhov have mentioned samovars, often using them as symbols of typical Russian domesticity.

Like the French, the everyday Russian did not drink tea with any regularity until the nineteenth century, but since then, the population of Russia and the rest of the former Soviet Union has acquired an insatiable appetite for it. Most of the tea consumed in Russia now is imported from India and Sri Lanka, although Chinese tea was the first tea brought into the country. During the long hard years of Stalin's regime, tea was regularly available, even when other staples such as flour and bread and certainly fresh meat and vegetables were not.

Russia has a long and romantic history of importing tea. Beginning in the seventeenth century, large overland caravans of hundreds of camels carried tea from China to Moscow, an arduous journey that took more than a year. This mode of transport limited the supply of tea, which meant only the nobility had the opportunity to enjoy it. Not until the opening of the Siberian railroad in 1880, which reduced the travel time for the tea to a matter of two short months, did the common person experience tea. From that time onward, however, it has been a mainstay of Russian daily life. No home was too humble for a samovar, which is still true today.

Samovars can be elegant or simple and are usually made of copper or bronze, although some are porcelain. Regardless of the material used to construct them, they are forever associated with Russian tea drinking—although the large kettlelike urn, with its charcoal-fired inner core for heating the water, was invented in China. Tea brewed in a small teapot nesting on top of the samovar is called *tscheinik* and is very strong and concentrated. No one drinks it without first diluting it with the water in the samovar, available through a spigot.

The Russian habit of drinking tea through a sugar cube or with a spoonful of jam is testimony to an independent spirit. Not only is each cup of tea diluted by each tea drinker to his (or her) own liking, but he (or she) decides whether to hold a sugar cube between the teeth, stir a spoonful of jam into the brew, or simply add a lemon slice to it. Certainly other cultures sweeten tea or soften its astringency with milk, but the Russian method is noisy and happily exuberant. Russians would no more think of adding milk to tea than they would consider omitting the lemon or sugar.

Although the *tscheinik* may be green or black tea, most often it is slightly smoked black tea, a flavor that appeals to the Russians, harking back to the days of the camel caravans. Then, the tea was natu-

The Perfect Cup for Tea

I always drink tea in thin-shelled cups with white interiors. I am not happy drinking from mugs. They are too thick and leave me with the sensation of being removed from the taste of the tea. The inside of the cup must be white so I can appreciate the color of the tea. I like looking at the "halo" or slightly lighter ring of color that encircles the beverage around the inside of the cup. However, as Lu Yu said, "In the end goodness is for the mouth to decide."

rally smoked by the time it arrived at its destination, having been held in chests that were exposed to nightly campfires during the long overland trek. Today, Russian Caravan tea is lightly smoked tea and should not be confused with Imperial Russian blended tea, which is flavored with bergamot.

Modern Russians consider tea as much a national beverage as vodka and drink it from morning to night. It is served with all meals and as a pick-me-up during the day. Unlike the Europeans, the Russians do not associate tea with any specific foods. To them, tea is simply part of life.

Tea in Australia

The residents of urban Australia tend to drink tea very similarly to the English. When they have the time and opportunity, they set aside an hour or so in the afternoon for tea and sweets. They consume black tea all day long and call their early evening supper "tea." For a truly down-under tea experience, one must travel to Australia's Outback, where the jackaroos and swaggies, the Aussie versions of the American cowboy and hobo, respectively, drink billy tea.

The famous song about Waltzing Matilda contains a line about the swaggie waiting for his billy to boil, indicating that billy tea is very much part of Australian folklore. Billy tea is made in a billy, which is nothing more than a tin can with a long handle fashioned from a length of wire. Into this makeshift kettle go the black tea leaves and water, which is then left to boil over the campfire. The crude tea is as much part of jackaroo lore as the coffeepot is of cowboy legend. The billy was (and still is in many parts of the continent) the first thing on the campfire at night, the hot tea meant to ward off the chill of the evening, and again the first pot grabbed in the morning. Strong, undoubtedly bitter billy tea fortified the jackaroo as he roamed the vast expanse of the Outback, tending to his cattle.

Billy tea may be a symbol of the jackaroo, but the swaggies are credited with inventing it. These tramps are known as swagmen or swaggies because of the ever-present "swag" hanging from the pole slung over their shoulders and holding their few worldly possessions. Without fail, tea leaves were wrapped inside the swag, and the swaggie, stopping under a bridge, along the railroad, or by the banks of a stream, mixed the precious leaves with anything else he could find to extend their life and sustain his. This might mean that the tea was mixed with twigs, leaves, or even insects. When the tea had brewed, turned a good, strong color, and, as tradition says, when the bacon was cooked and ready to eat, the swaggie would "swing the billy."

Swinging the billy was important because it is by this method that the tea is separated from the leaves and rendered suitable for drinking. The billy was held by the long handle and with a quick heave, swung windmill fashion—just as children playfully swing pails full of sand and sea water at the beach—so that the centrifugal pull settled the leaves on the bottom of the can and the liquor could be poured into mugs.

Unless they were on the move, both swaggies and jackaroos left billy tea simmering on campfires all day long. In the evening, the fire was built up, the strong tea once again brought to a full boil, and more tea leaves added to the billy. By now, the tea was a ferocious brew that could be tamed with a judicious spoonful of sugar—although more often than not it was drunk unsweetened. Real jackaroos don't add sugar!

Living a rough-and-tumble existence does not lend itself to specialized culinary treats. Dampers were frequently all that these men had to eat with billy tea. Made from simple batters of flour and water and baked directly in the embers or in a skillet, dampers are about as basic a bread as exists. Any vegetables or meat that might be on hand could be stirred into the bread batter, although if times were hard, a coating of ashes from the fire was the only flavoring.

Onion and Pepper Damper

SERVES 10 TO 12

Olive oil, for oiling the skillet

3 cups all-purpose flour

1 tablespoon baking powder

2 teaspoons salt

½ cup finely chopped onions

½ cup finely diced red bell peppers

½ cup finely diced yellow bell peppers

Preheat the oven to 425°F. Lightly oil a 9- or 10-inch cast-iron skillet with olive oil.

In a mixing bowl, combine the flour, baking powder, and salt and mix with a wooden spoon. Add the onions and peppers and mix well. Make a shallow well in the center of the mixture and add 1½ cups of water. Mix the dough with the wooden spoon or your hands until it is uniformly moistened.

Spoon the dough into the skillet and, using moistened hands, press it evenly into the pan. Bake for 20 to 25 minutes or until firm to the touch. Run a knife around the edge of the damper to loosen it and remove in one piece to a wire rack to cool. Serve warm or at room temperature.

Tea in the United States

Although Americans still consume far more coffee and coffee products than tea, tea remains one of our largest imports. This is testament to our long association with the beverage, which began in the 1600s when Dutch traders made sure the colonists had tea for their larders. These settlers loved their tea, and so, when the English attempted to control the market in an effort to bolster the fortunes of the flagging East India Company, the restless colonists revolted. In 1773, a group of patriots dressed like Native Americans boarded the English ships anchored in Boston Harbor and tossed three hundred forty-two chests of tea into the bay, a dramatic gesture that became known as the Boston Tea Party. More "tea parties" followed in other ports, clear acts of defiance against a government that was becoming intolerable to many of its subjects in the New World. Three short years later, in 1776, the Declaration of Independence was signed.

After independence, Americans still clung to tea as part of their daily diet, despite a brief period when it was shunned as being "too British." In the 1800s, tea was considered an integral part of society, indicating an appreciation for the finer things in life, ironically as interpreted by English custom. Afternoon tea and English-style tea dances were *de rigueur* among the upper classes, who, as the century progressed, became increasingly insular. However, not only the rich drank tea. Common Americans loved it. Knowing how to prepare and serve it was considered a mark of good manners, despite social class. The tea trade made some Americans rich, which helped establish other industries and in turn gave rise to that great American social experiment: the middle class.

The tea trade was responsible for a glorious if short period of American navigational history when fast, sleek Yankee clipper ships enabled American merchants to trade directly with the Chinese, carrying cargo to both England and America. These handsome three-masted ships, with names such as *Flying Cloud*, *Argonaut*, and *White Squall* were unequaled for speed, and so increased the chance that the precious tea leaves would reach their designation before they spoiled. The glamorous clippers captured the imaginations of nearly everyone, epitomizing the romance of life on the high seas where it was possible to visit strange and distant ports, have exotic adventures, and come home with an eagerly awaited cargo. The British built their own clipper ships, competing directly with the Americans for speed on the oceans, although American clippers were always considered superior. It became good sport in both countries to track the progress of these ships and even to lay wagers on their success. After barely more than a decade, steady, reliable steamships replaced clippers as the ships of choice for the tea trade, but the clippers' allure and lore lingered long and remains a cherished part of the nation's maritime history.

Iced tea, which was introduced at the 1904 St. Louis World's Fair, was not the only tea innovation introduced during the twentieth century. New York tea merchant Thomas Sullivan marketed tea in silk pouches, precursors to the now widely used tea bags. These two variants from the long-held practices of steeping tea from leaves and serving it piping hot changed the course of tea history nearly as significantly as had the early trade routes. Tea bags were an instant success, appealing to a population that was increasingly on the move, and putting tea on portable coffee carts, in diners, cafeterias, and every home—albeit often nesting in the back of a cupboard. But

Iced Tea and Ice Cream Cones

Until the turn of the twentieth century, Americans had drunk only tea from China and had an abiding fondness for green tea as well as Chinese black tea. An enterprising English tea merchant named Richard Blechynden decided to introduce black Indian tea to Americans, and so he set up a booth at the 1904 St. Louis World's Fair. The summer weather was uncomfortably hot and humid, and few fair goers wanted to try a cup of hot, steaming tea. Blechynden dropped some ice into the tea and "discovered" a wonderfully refreshing drink perfect for sipping in sweltering weather. Iced tea was born. It is interesting to note that this same fair gave rise to other cherished all-American culinary treats. Waffle vendors rolled waffles into cones and set scoops of ice cream in the openings; sausage sellers put their long wursts on split rolls. The invention of the ice cream cone and the hot dog allowed people to hold the food in their hands as they strolled through the fair grounds—a novel experience for the times. These and iced tea were the talk of the Fair, and its three tastiest legacies.

they also gave tea companies the opportunity to use inferior tea. Crushed fannings and tea dust often ended up in these bags (and still do)—who could tell through the paper envelope?—and this profitable practice became commonplace with some manufacturers. This is a shame, because it meant that American tea became associated with poor-quality tea. However, this did not seem to bother the Americans. Leaf tea, brewed with fancy utensils and served with indulgent pastries, was considered a luxury of the upper classes. The democratic middle class could not be bothered. American ingenuity won out over flavor and tradition.

Iced tea was especially popular in the southern states, where it was usually mixed with sugar and sometimes a little lemon. Today, it's difficult in many southern restaurants to get "unsweetened tea," and upon entering many down-home southern establishments, customers are welcomed with a large, frosty pitcher of sweet iced tea. America's growing appreciation of iced tea gave rise to powdered iced-tea mixes. These shelf-stable products barely resemble tea, but are nonetheless popular throughout the country. More recently, the tea trade in the United States received a boost with the introduction of canned and bottled iced-tea drinks.

These products are, to a purveyor of fine tea, an anathema. However, I have been heartened by a small but steady renaissance in America. Splendid tea emporiums are opening across the nation offering fine teas, educating their customers to the differences among teas, and offering updated and interesting blends.

Tea in Arabia

Since traders first carried tea leaves out of China for overland trade, tea has been important to the countries of Arabia, although in modern terms, its spread was gradual. Serving and drinking tea is an essential part of Arab culture, with tea rituals combining the practical and symbolic.

Although customs differ from country to country, both green and black tea are drunk in Arab countries. Green tea is common in Morocco and Afghanistan, while black tea is drunk in other countries. In Morocco, the tea is made by first pouring a small amount of boiling water over the green tea leaves and immediately discarding the water to rid the leaves of any bitterness. Next, mint leaves are added. Using a small hammer, usually made of copper, the tea maker taps a sizable chunk of sugar from a sugar loaf and adds it to the pot with the mint and tea. Finally more boiling water is added, and the pot is covered with a lid or a fine linen napkin and left to steep. Family members and guests are expected to take these few moments of steeping for quiet reflection and private thoughts. The lid is removed from the teapot, and the tea is stirred and tasted. The host then adjusts the amount of sugar and mint and finally pours the tea. Even pouring is stylized, as the hot, minty beverage is poured from a height that shows off the clarity of the tea and lets its aroma fill the immediate area. In the days when many Moroccans were desert nomads, the moment when the tent filled with the intoxicating aroma of freshly made mint tea must have been magical. During meals, guests are served three glasses of this *shai b'nanah*, which satisfies the taste buds and acts as digestive aid, necessary in a country where delectable dishes such as couscous and rich tangines are served in generous amounts.

In Morocco, tea is served by the head of the household or by the eldest son as a rite of passage into manhood, but never by women or servants. Making the tea is considered a responsibility and honor in these homes and as such is reserved for the men in the family.

Pouring tea for guests is also viewed as a tribute to Allah, and therefore is pivotal to daily life. Through the ages, Arabs have never left home without their prayer mats, prayer beads, and a teapot. Particularly in the past, the teapot doubled as a receptacle for cool, clean water used for the five daily ablutions performed before Muslim prayers and devotions.

Egyptians drink so much tea that the government subsidizes it to keep prices reasonable. These North Africans drink it all day long—and have been at least since the fifteenth century—making Egypt one of the largest black tea–importing countries in the world. Egyptians prefer their tea strong, sweetened with sugar, and sometimes served with a glass of cold water.

In Turkey tea has been a staple of the population since Turkish traders bartered for bricks of tea on the Mongolian border in the fifth century A.D., and is drunk far more frequently than coffee. Known as *demlikacay*, making the tea is the responsibility of the woman of the house. Women scrutinize prospective daughters-in-law to determine if their tea-making skills are up to snuff. Black tea is kept hot all day long in nested teapots called *cay danlik* and permitted to get very strong. It is then poured into glasses and diluted with hot water. The Turks appreciate sweets with their tea, and the bakeries up and down the Bosporus Strait sell tasty confections.

Yogurt Pistachio Cake

SERVES 8 TO 10

Unsalted butter, for buttering the pan

1 ⅔ cups all-purpose flour

2 teaspoons baking powder

¼ teaspoon salt

1 cup plain yogurt (see Note)

1 teaspoon baking soda

½ cup (1 stick) unsalted butter, at room temperature

1 cup granulated sugar

2 large eggs

3 tablespoons fresh lemon juice

Grated zest of 1 lemon

1 cup shelled, skinned pistachio nuts, coarsely chopped

Confectioners' sugar

Preheat the oven to 350°F. Butter and flour a 9-inch round cake pan. Tap out the excess flour.

Sift together the flour, baking powder, and salt and set aside.

In a separate bowl, stir the yogurt with the baking soda.

Using an electric mixer set on medium-high speed, cream the room-temperature butter until light. Add the sugar and beat for about 5 minutes until the batter is light and fluffy. Add the eggs, 1 at a time, incorporating the first egg before adding the second. With the mixer set on low, add the dry ingredients, one-third at a time, alternating with half the yogurt mixture and ending with the dry ingredients. Add the lemon juice and beat for 1 minute. Fold in the lemon zest and pistachio nuts. Scrape the batter into the pan and bake on the center rack of the oven for 35 to 40 minutes or until golden brown and the edges pull away from the sides of the pan.

Let the cake cool in the pan for a few minutes before turning out onto a wire rack to cool completely. Dust with confectioners' sugar and serve.

Note: Use regular plain yogurt, not low-fat or nonfat yogurt.

Turkish Macaroons

MAKES 14 SANDWICHED COOKIES; 28 SINGLE COOKIES

3 cups sliced blanched almonds

2 cups granulated sugar

4 large egg whites

2 teaspoons almond extract

Position the oven racks in the upper and lower thirds of the oven. Preheat the oven to 350°F. Line 2 baking sheets with parchment or wax paper.

In a food processor, combine the almonds and 6 tablespoons of the sugar and process until finely ground. Add the egg whites and extract and process for about 20 seconds or until smooth. Add the remaining sugar, pulse for 8 to 10 seconds, scrape down the sides of the bowl, and continue processing until well mixed.

With moistened fingers, pinch off walnut-sized pieces of dough and roll into balls between moistened palms. Place the balls on the baking sheets, leaving about 2 inches between them. Flatten the balls slightly.

Bake for 12 minutes and then reverse the positions of the baking sheets, so that the one on the top oven rack is now on the lower rack, and vice versa. Bake for 12 to 13 minutes longer until the cookies are golden brown.

continued

Remove the baking sheets from the oven and immediately raise one end of the parchment paper. Carefully pour 1/4 cup of cold water under the parchment paper on each sheet, tilting the baking sheets so that the water spreads over the surface of the hot pans and under the sheets of paper. When the water stops bubbling, carefully peel the macaroons from the paper and cool on wire racks. For sandwiched cookies, assemble pairs of the still-warm cookies and press the flat sides together. Let them cool completely.

In Iraq, black tea is served in teahouses that curiously are often referred to as coffeehouses. Here, as in other countries in the region, the tea is served in small glasses and with sweet pastries filled with nuts, dried fruit, and dates. The Iraqis also like tisanes for their medicinal properties, which is logical for the population of a country where medical supplies are scarce.

In both Iran and Afghanistan, tea is drunk Russian style, using a samovar to heat the water and keep the teapot hot, and with the same frequency as in Russia. The Afghans drink cup after cup of black or green tea in rustic teahouses called *chaikhana* where townspeople gather to share gossip and listen to local musicians and singers. In both the *chaikhana* and private homes, tea is served in ceramic or porcelain cups rather than the glasses found in nearby countries. Black tea is traditionally served for warmth, while green tea is enjoyed for its flavor and as a thirst quencher.

Tea in India and Sri Lanka

Although India is a major tea-producing country, its tea customs are not entrenched in ritual. This most likely is because the Indians only began drinking tea in the nineteenth century when the British established tea estates to satisfy their particular appetite for the drink.

As they go about their daily business, Indians drink milky black tea morning, noon, and night, buying tea in disposable terra-cotta cups from industrious street vendors. Visitors to India immediately notice the tea sellers at the bustling train stations, calling out "*Cha!*" or "*Cha-ya*," regardless of the hour. Train station tea is one of the pleasures of Indian train travel, which can be arduous, as it revives and soothes the weary traveler.

Cha-ya, Indian street tea, is boiled in an open kettle and is often spiced with cardamom seeds, fennel, and sugar. Milk is added to the boiling brew, in a ratio of about one part milk for every four parts of tea. While this beverage is peddled throughout the vast subcontinent, it is more common in the north. Residents of south India prefer coffee. Street tea may be ubiquitous in India, but it is not representative of the fine teas grown in the country.

Tea is also served in the British style in some hotels in the large cities and resort towns. This custom was introduced by the British during the era of the Raj, when the tea planters and military families insisted on enjoying afternoon tea in the steamy tropics—a stubborn habit that still conjures up fairly comical images of overdressed Europeans being served hot tea on airless verandahs. However, the custom was not completely English. The teapots and cups were as likely to be of Indian design as of English, which meant bright colors and fanciful shapes. Both the English and Indians like savory food with tea as well as sweets, often indulging in a platter of samosas, vadas, or some crisp, peppery bread.

Potato Vada

MAKES 10 PATTIES

2 pounds boiling potatoes, peeled and cut into chunks

¼ cup finely minced scallions

2 tablespoons chopped fresh mint

1 tablespoon minced jalapeño pepper

1½ teaspoons finely minced fresh ginger

Salt and freshly ground black pepper

Vegetable oil, for frying

1 large egg, lightly beaten

Plain dried bread crumbs

Boil the potatoes in salted water for 15 to 20 minutes until tender. Drain and return to the pan or transfer to a mixing bowl. Using a potato masher or fork, mash the potatoes until smooth. Stir in the scallions, mint, jalapeño, and ginger and season to taste with salt and pepper. Set aside to cool slightly.

Pour oil into a deep-fat fryer or large, deep skillet to a depth of 2 to 3 inches. Heat over high heat to 350°F.

Put the egg in a shallow dish and the bread crumbs in another.

With moistened hands, form the mashed potatoes into patties about 1-inch thick and 2½-inches wide. Dip the patties into the egg and then the bread crumbs to coat, and then, using a slotted metal spoon, submerge in the hot oil. Fry the patties, several at a time, for 2 or 3 minutes or until golden brown. Let the oil regain its temperature between batches. Drain on paper towels and serve warm.

Notes: The fried patties can be kept warm in a warm (200°F) oven for 15 or 20 minutes.

The patties can be baked rather than fried. To bake the patties, place them on a lightly oiled baking sheet and bake them in a preheated 450°F oven for about 10 minutes on each side.

Nimki

SERVES 4 TO 6

1 cup all-purpose flour

1 tablespoon sesame seeds

1 teaspoon cumin seeds

½ teaspoon toasted cumin seeds

½ teaspoon toasted coriander seeds, lightly crushed

½ teaspoon salt

¼ teaspoon cayenne pepper

¼ teaspoon baking powder

1 tablespoon vegetable oil

Vegetable oil, for frying

In a mixing bowl, combine the flour, sesame seeds, cumin seeds, coriander seeds, salt, cayenne, baking powder, and tablespoon of vegetable oil and stir until combined. Add ⅓ cup of water and mix to form a stiff dough.

Knead the dough a few times in the bowl and then turn the dough out onto a lightly floured work surface and divide the dough in half. Working with 1 piece of dough at a time, roll the dough into a very thin rectangle. Cut the dough into strips about 4 inches long and ¼ inch wide. Set aside and roll out the other half of dough and make more strips.

Pour oil into a deep-fat fryer or large, deep skillet to a depth of 2 to 3 inches. Heat over high heat to 350°F. Fry the strips in batches for 2 or

3 minutes until golden brown. Drain on paper towels. Serve warm or at room temperature.

Lovely, tropical Sri Lanka, the land where world-famous Ceylon tea is grown, is not a major tea-drinking nation, although its major agricultural crop is tea, followed by coconuts. In the more populated areas, drinking tea is considered a sign of wealth and prestige, and the tea is served in the British style, often complete with a silver tea service. In rural areas, tea is served more casually.

Sri Lankans drink tea with breakfast, but then generally don't indulge again until the end of the day, when they may gather at home to recline on large pillows and sip a cup, or congregate in tea gardens tucked into the lush foliage of the tea estates and terraced slopes of the hills. This is a time for catching up on local news, sipping ambrosial black tea, and perhaps sampling a simple sweet or two.

Coconut Roti

SERVES 6

2 cups all-purpose flour

¾ cup shredded sweetened or unsweetened coconut (see Note)

1 teaspoon salt

Vegetable oil, for frying

In a mixing bowl, combine the flour, coconut, and salt and whisk 8 to 10 times until mixed. Make a shallow well in the center of the dry ingredients and add 1 cup of water. Using a wooden spoon, stir until a soft dough forms. It should not be sticky.

Turn the dough onto a lightly floured work surface and knead for about 5 minutes until smooth. Put the dough in a clean, dry bowl, cover with plastic wrap, and let rest for about 30 minutes.

Heat a cast-iron skillet or griddle over medium heat. Pour a little oil onto a crumpled paper towel and rub the oil over the hot skillet or griddle.

Divide the dough into 6 equal-sized pieces, lay them on the work surface, and cover with a clean, dry kitchen towel. Working with 1 piece at a time, flatten the dough into a 6-inch-diameter disk and fry 1 to 1½ minutes until the bottom is golden. Turn and fry about 1 minute longer until golden. Wrap the roti in a dry kitchen towel to keep warm while forming and frying the rest. Rub the skillet or

continued

griddle with more oil as necessary. Serve warm or at room temperature.

Note: Tradition calls for unsweetened shredded coconut, but sweetened is far easier to find and produces an equally delicious roti with a little more sweetness.

Tea in Myanmar

In this country that used to be Burma, the teapot is the actual and metaphorical center of social life and stands as symbol of unity and harmony. At tea stalls found throughout this nation, which shares borders with India and China to the northwest and northeast and with Thailand to the south, the Myanmarese gather to "tea-shop sit" and discuss local and regional politics with characteristic vigor. Here the term "green tea circle" refers to a group dedicated to serious conversation about the weightier issues of the day.

Myanmar boasts a long history of tea drinking, which is not surprising given its proximity to China. However, depending on the legend you choose to believe, tea was not drunk with any regularity in Burma until either the twelfth or fourteenth century, which, of course, is long after the Chinese were enjoying it.

The Myanmarese have a peculiar habit of eating pickled tea leaves that are served with delicacies such as dried shrimp, sesame seeds, roasted beans, and fried garlic. Although these leaves are not infused into tea, they are offered as symbols of hospitality, just as is hot liquid tea.

Today's population is torn between the traditions of the past and the allure of the future and all its capitalist trappings. However, nearly all citizens, young or old, prefer their tea sweet and strong, and even have a term, *kyaukpadaung*, which means *very* strong and *very* sweet tea, which they like to serve with sweet pastries and puddings. When the tea is made with imported condensed milk, it is considered a luxury and becomes *she*, or special.

Coconut Semolina Pudding

SERVES 12

1 cup coarse semolina

2 cups unsweetened coconut cream

1 cup granulated sugar

1 vanilla bean, split

4 tablespoons unsalted butter, at room temperature

¼ teaspoon salt

¼ teaspoon cardamom

3 large eggs, separated

⅓ cup sweetened coconut, plus ⅛ cup for sprinkling

Preheat the oven to 325°F. Lightly butter a 9-inch square baking pan.

Put the semolina in a saucepan off the heat. Whisk in the coconut cream and 1 cup of water until there are no lumps. Stir in the sugar and then scrape the vanilla bean seeds into the mixture. Bring the mixture to a boil over high heat, stirring constantly. When the mixture starts to bubble and thicken slightly, add the butter, a tablespoon at a time, not adding the next tablespoon until the preceding one is incorporated. Stir in the salt and cardamom.

Using an electric mixer set on medium speed, beat the egg whites until foamy. Increase the speed to high and beat until stiff peaks form.

Add the yolks to the pudding mixture, 1 at a time, not adding the next yolk until the preceding yolk is incorporated. Gently fold in the egg whites and ⅓ cup of coconut. Scrape the pudding into the prepared pan and sprinkle the remaining ⅛ cup of coconut over the top. Bake for 50 to 60 minutes until the top is golden brown and the pudding is set. Cool in the pan before cutting into squares for serving.

The Chinese revere and admire the tea they produce and for thousands of years have been perfecting the art of drinking it. They do not engage in complicated tea ceremonies, as do the Japanese, but instead drink tea at home and in teahouses. The latter are rustic or elegant but their primary focus is to serve tea and tea alone. The important point to remember is that the Chinese drink tea all day, every day, and have incorporated it into every aspect of life, serious, light-hearted, or somber.

Tibetan Tea

High in the Himalayas, Tibetans make their own special kind of tea from the compressed brick tea, the precursor to tuo-cha. *This is an earthy tea with a pleasing if perhaps unusual aroma of soil. Because of the compressed shape, it is convenient to transport, even in the most treacherous terrain. The Tibetans boil tea all night so that by morning it is extremely strong. They then churn it with salt and yak butter into a thick, rich brew that, once you try it, is evidently quite addictive. Tibetans, who consider tea essential to hospitality, also make this tea with goat's milk.*

Mongols make a tea similar to tuo-cha, *using mare's milk. I market a* tuo-cha pu'erh *tea, which is one of the only teas I like mixed with milk.*

Kung Fu

This Chinese tea practice promotes equality. Maoist in philosophy, the egalitarian ceremony is also sometimes called gong fu *to distinguish it from the martial art. Either way, it means "to do well." Utensils are simple: a small Yixing pot made to hold only six or eight ounces of tea and a set of small handleless cups with saucers. The cups, which hold no more than a thimbleful of tea, are arranged in a circle on a tray or in a shallow bowl, rims touching. Boiling water is poured over the cups and into the pot to warm them up and then discarded. The water is returned to the boil while tea leaves—usually oolong—are measured into the pot. (I personally favor Pi Lo Chun tea for this ceremony.)*

The ritual involves pouring a little boiling water over the leaves in the pot to rinse them, pouring it off, letting the water return to the boil, and then making the tea. When the water is added to the leaves to infuse the tea, the host is supposed to take four deep breaths (which should take about thirty seconds) before he pours the tea.

Pouring is the most important part of kung fu, as it symbolizes true equality. The host pours the tea in a continuous stream, rotating the pot in a circle over the cups until no tea remains in the pot and the cups are equally filled. This means that no one person gets more or less tea than any other and that all taste tea of equal strength. The same leaves can be used again with more boiling water; superstition decrees that the more times the leaves are reused, the luckier the tea drinkers will be.

Zhongs

These ingenious, lidded Chinese teacups enable tea drinkers to sip tea using the lids as shields against the tea leaves in the cups. In rural provinces and in bustling cities, the Chinese use these sensible vessels to infuse a single cup and to drink their tea without the fuss of straining the tea leaves. It's common to see people carrying zhongs *with them to offices or into the fields. They are also used in teahouses when the tea is steeped in individual cups right at the table. When the customer removes the lid, waiters know to bring him some more boiling water to pour over the tea leaves.*

Before communism gripped China in the middle of the twentieth century, teahouses were found on every main thoroughfare and back street in large cities and small towns. Mao Zedong's government attempted to close the teahouses, believing they encouraged idleness. However, so important had they been to Chinese daily life for centuries, they were never completely expunged, and in recent decades, as China has become more open to the world, these establishments have experienced a welcome revitalization.

The Chinese drink green, white, and oolong tea and only rarely drink black tea. How each is steeped is important to them. They fill clay pots or *zhongs* (lidded cups with saucers) nearly halfway with tea leaves and then add a small measure of very hot water. This is quickly poured off, its purpose being to heat the pot and wash the leaves. Water of the same temperature is again poured over the tea and the tea is allowed to infuse for the length of time appropriate for its type: Green tea is steeped for less time that oolong tea. Green and white teas sometimes are infused two or three times, while oolongs and blacks (when drunk) can be infused as many as five times.

While no food is served at teahouses, the Chinese enjoy food with their tea when they eat at home and in restaurants. Both savories and sweets are appropriate when drinking Chinese green, white, or oolong teas; smoked teas such as Lapsang Souchong are best served with spicy foods such as those from the provinces of Szechwan and Hunan.

Ginger-Almond Precious Pudding

SERVES 10

1/4 cup currants

2 cups glutinous rice (see Note)

3/4 cup granulated sugar

2 tablespoons canola oil

10 whole toasted almonds

1/4 cup candied kumquats, coarsely chopped (see Note)

1/4 cup crystallized ginger, coarsely chopped

1/4 cup toasted almonds, coarsely chopped

1 cup red bean paste (see Note)

Lightly oil a 7-inch-diameter heatproof bowl.

Put the currants in a bowl, add boiling water to cover, and let sit for 10 minutes to plump. Drain and set aside.

Rinse the rice several times in cold water until the water runs clear. Transfer the rice to a saucepan, add 2 cups of water and let sit for 30 minutes.

Bring the rice to a boil over high heat, cover, reduce the heat to low, and cook for about 20 minutes until the water is absorbed and the rice is tender. Remove from the heat and let rest for 10 minutes. Stir in the sugar and canola oil.

Arrange the whole almonds in the bottom of the heatproof bowl in a decorative fashion. Sprinkle a little less than half the currants, kumquats, ginger, and chopped almonds in the bowl, also decoratively. Stir the remaining currants, kumquats, ginger, and chopped almonds into the rice.

Spoon half the rice into the bowl, taking care not to disturb the nuts and fruit. With moistened hands, press the rice gently into the bowl. Spread the red bean paste in an even layer over the rice. Add the remaining rice and spread it over the bean paste. Cover the bowl with aluminum foil.

Pour enough water into a wok or large, deep pot to measure about 2 inches. Set a bamboo steamer or wire rack in the wok or pot. Bring the water to a simmer over medium-high heat. Place the bowl on the steamer or rack, cover the larger vessel, and steam for about 1 hour or until the pudding is set. Add more hot water to the wok or pot during steaming as needed. Lift the bowl from the larger vessel and run a knife around the outside of the pudding to release it. Set a plate over the bowl and, holding the plate securely, invert the bowl. Lift the bowl from the pudding and serve the pudding warm or at room temperature.

Note: Glutinous rice, candied kumquats, and red bean paste are available at Asian markets. Chop the kumquats, crystallized ginger, and almonds after measuring.

Steamed Buns with Red Bean Paste

MAKES 16 BUNS

2¼ cups bleached all-purpose flour

¼ cup granulated sugar

3½ teaspoons baking powder

6 tablespoons milk

3 tablespoons peanut oil

1 cup red bean paste (see Note)

In a mixing bowl, stir together the flour, sugar, and baking powder. Make a shallow well in the center of the dry ingredients and add the milk, oil, and 6 tablespoons of water. Stir with a wooden spoon until the liquid is absorbed and the dough holds together in a mass. On a lightly floured surface, knead the dough for about 10 minutes or until the dough is smooth and elastic. Transfer to a clean bowl, cover with plastic wrap, and let rest for 1 hour.

Cut sixteen 2½-inch squares of wax paper.

Divide the dough in half and return one half to the bowl and cover. Cut the other half of the dough into 8 pieces. Working with 1 piece of dough at a time, roll the dough on a lightly floured surface into a 4- or 5-inch circle. Spoon a scant tablespoon of bean paste into the center of the dough circle, and gather the dough up and around the filling, making tiny pleats in the dough and then twisting it gently closed. Set the bun on a square of wax paper. Repeat with the

Yum Cha and Finger Tapping

When I lived in Melbourne, Australia, I always considered it a great treat to eat Yum Cha at a Chinese restaurant in Chinatown, an experience similar to eating the dim sum that Americans enjoy. I would often notice that the older Chinese tapped three fingers of one of their hands. This finger tapping is, apparently, a silent ritual of appreciation and gratitude stemming from the legend of a Qing Dynasty emperor who would travel among his subjects anonymously. While on such an outing, the emperor visited a teahouse and, to preserve his anonymity, took his turn at pouring tea. His entourage, wanting to kowtow for the honor being bestowed upon them, was instructed to tap, simultaneously, one finger for the bowed head and two more for their prostrate arms, thus enabling them to kowtow without revealing the emperor's identity.

remaining dough. When all eight pieces are used, cover them with a clean, dry kitchen towel. Remove the other half of the dough from the bowl and repeat the process for a total of 16 buns.

Pour enough water into a wok or large, deep pot to measure about 2 inches. Set a bamboo steamer or wire rack in the wok or pot. Bring the water to a simmer over medium-high heat. Place the buns, still on the squares of wax paper, on the steamer or rack, cover the larger vessel, and steam for 15 to 20 minutes until the buns are firm and shiny. Serve warm.

Note: Red bean paste is available at Asian markets.

Sesame Seed Cookies

MAKES ABOUT 96 COOKIES

2 cups bleached all-purpose flour

1 teaspoon baking powder

¼ teaspoon salt

¾ cup granulated sugar

¼ pound (1 stick) unsalted butter, at room temperature

1 large egg

1 teaspoon almond extract

1 teaspoon pure vanilla extract

1 cup toasted sesame seeds (see Notes)

In a bowl, combine the flour, baking powder, and salt and whisk 8 to 10 times.

Using an electric mixer set on medium-high speed, cream the sugar and butter until light and fluffy. Add the egg and extracts and mix until blended. Add the dry ingredients and mix until thoroughly blended. Lay a piece of plastic wrap on a work surface and scrape the dough onto it. Using your hands and the plastic wrap as guides, form the dough into a log about 12 inches long and 2 inches in diameter. Wrap securely and refrigerate for at least 2 hours until firm.

Preheat the oven to 375°F. Lightly butter 2 baking sheets. Spread the sesame seeds on a flat plate or dish.

Unwrap the dough and cut it into ⅛-inch-thick slices. Press one side of the slices into the sesame seeds so that the seeds adhere to the dough. Lay the slices, seed-covered sides up, on the baking sheets, leaving about an inch between cookies. Bake for 8 to 10 minutes or until the bottoms are golden. Let cool on the baking sheets for a few minutes and then cool completely on wire racks. Repeat until all the cookies are baked.

Notes: To toast the sesame seeds, spread them in a dry skillet and cook over medium heat, stirring, for 3 or 4 minutes until the seeds are golden and fragrant. Slide onto a plate to cool.

If you do not want to make all 96 cookies at one time, wrap the unused portion of the log in plastic wrap and aluminum foil and freeze it for up to 1 month. Let it defrost in the refrigerator and then bake as instructed.

"Tea is nothing other than this: Heat the water, prepare the tea, and drink with propriety; that is all you need to know." These words still apply today in Japan. They are attributed to Rikyu, considered by many to be the most influental Japanese tea master and teacher, or *sen*, and were spoken in the sixteenth century. How well this advice fits with Zen teachings, a philosophy with no complicated intentions or implications, which, when practiced properly, reveals pure thought in its most natural environment.

The Japanese have elevated the tea ceremony to an art form that is acknowleged by the rest of the world, but rarely understood. Essentially, the ritual is an aesthetic experience with the goal of evoking relaxation and appreciation for all that is pure, beautiful, and serene.

Sen Rikyu is also reported to have advised disciples to do the following when preparing tea: "Make a delicious bowl of tea. Distribute the charcoal evenly so as to heat the water just so. Arrange the flowers the way they grow in the field. In summer, suggest coolness; in winter, warmth. Anticipate everything; be ready for rain if it comes. Show the greatest consideration toward your guest."

Consideration of one's guests is at the center of the *Cha-no-yu* tea ceremony, a ritual that has survived the centuries. However, today few Japanese outside of monasteries practice it in its pure form—although all modern Japanese know the phrase and understand it to one degree or another.

During the traditional ceremony there are "only the host, his guest, and the tea," said Sen Rikyu. The ceremony takes place in a *sukiya*, a special room or space set aside for tea, and the adjoining *rōji*, the garden. Those who can afford it build a separate *sukiya* or teahouse, and others set aside an area of the house for the ceremony. This should be the size of four by four and a half tatami mats and partitioned from the rest of the house with a screen—an arrangement called a *kakoi*, or enclosure.

The *sukiya* must be simply decorated to the point of austerity so as not to influence the balance of the mind. Japanese build their teahouses from available materials so as not to put undue significance on material things.

When the ceremony begins, guests walk through the garden and are greeted in silence by the host, who invites them to rinse their mouths and hands in a small basin. This ritual of purification is performed before the guests enter the *sukiya* through a small entrance called a *nijiri-agari*, which is less than two feet wide and only a little higher, requiring guests to humble themselves as they enter the *sukiya*. The host enters the room through a larger door called the *katte-guchi* (back entrance) or *cha-tate-guchi* (tea maker's entrance).

During the first phase of the ceremony, called the *zenseki*, no more than four guests wait in the central room and contemplate a scroll with a saying or poem selected by the host. The number is limited because the number five represents the perfection integrated into a whole as defined by the five qualities of knowledge named by Buddha.

The host enters the room for the next phase, the *nakadachi*. He offers his guests a light meal called a *kaiseki*, with the food coming either from the mountains or the sea. Seated on tatami mats, the guests savor the food with their eyes and hearts, as well as their mouths, eating it with freshly cut bamboo chopsticks. The *kaiseki*

Interpreting the Japanese Tea Ceremony for the Twenty-first Century

I have adapted the seven rules for proper tea drinking first developed by Rikyu, the great sixteenth-century tea master who taught the Japanese the true meaning of Teaism. This meaning is as much meant to ensure serenity as a good cup of tea. For a description of the ritualized and formal Japanese tea ceremony, see to page 122.

1. The Tearoom:

Select a room or area of the house to be the sukiya *or* kakoi, *or tearoom. This should be a plain, unadorned space appropriate for quiet contemplation. Place in it a graceful vase with a few fresh-cut, fragrant flowers, such as orchids or lilies, or set a single, lovely piece of pottery in the room.*

2. The Tea:

This should be only the highest-quality green tea. Price should not be an issue since you will use only one teaspoon for every six-ounce cup of tea. For purity of taste and aroma remember that an unblended varietal is preferable to a blend.

3. The Water:

Use only fresh, cold water. If the tap water is sweet enough to use, let it run for a minute or so to aerate it. If you prefer bottled water, pour it into another container or through a filter to oxygenate it and give life to the tea. Fragile green tea requires water that is gently boiling—not yet at the rolling-boil pitch, which is preferred for black tea. The temperature of the water affects the reaction between the tea leaves and the water and can influence the taste and aroma of the tea.

4. **The Teapot:**

Select a porcelain or glass teapot. Rinse the pot with some boiling water, pour out the water, and then immediately spoon the measured amount of tea into the pot. Take a moment to appreciate the fragrant steam rising from the pot.

5. **The Infusion:**

The minute it boils, pour the water over leaves so that they begin steeping. This process is whimsically known as the "agony of the leaves." Steeping time for black teas is three to five minutes, but for green tea, it ranges from thirty seconds to three minutes, at most. Regardless of the type of tea, the threshold for steeping is five minutes, after which time the elements that contribute to its delightful astringency conspire to turn the tea bitter. Green tea is naturally more astringent than black tea and therefore should be watched even more carefully to insure it does not steep too long.

6. **The Pouring:**

In modern times, the tea is made using leaves, although in traditional and formal tea ceremonies, the tea is powdered. The leaves can be strained using a porcelain, bamboo, or stainless steel strainer that is set over the cup to capture the moist, plump leaves. Pour the tea slowly through the strainer and then discard the leaves.

7. **The Experience:**

Savor the tea as you would a glass of wine. Sip it slowly, inhale the aroma, and notice the delicate color. Between sips, gaze at the flowers or pottery, meditate on the principles of tea that long ago were established by Sen Rikyu as being harmony, reverence, purity, and calm.

The Japanese Hearth

Water for the Japanese tea ceremony of Cha-no-yu *is boiled over a charcoal fire, which must be maintained at an even heat to do justice to the tea water. In summer, the fire is built in a* furo, *a portable stove. In the winter, it is built in a small hearth cut directly into the floor of the teahouse. Upon the* furo *or hearth sits a* gotoku, *or trivet, to hold the kettle. Japanese tea kettles are of different shapes and sizes and usually are named after their region of origin.*

concludes with a sweet *namagushi*, which might be syrup-drenched pastry or sweetened white bean paste. Any conversation during the meal must be kept light and general, and when the food is finished, the guests return to the garden for a walk and fresh air.

Upon their return to the *sukiya*, tea is served. The scroll is replaced by flowers and tea-making utensils are arranged in readiness for the *tamae*, the actual making and serving of tea. These include a lacquered tea caddy (or *natsume*), scoop, bowl, and a whisk. The host scoops Matcha tea for each guest into the bowl and then adds boiling water, whisking the tea until it thickens slightly. This point is the height of the ceremony, after which the tea is sipped by everyone in a polite fashion. The utensils are then rinsed and dried and the most honored guest requests to examine the caddy and scoop, showing them to the other guests. The host leaves the room while his guests examine the utensils. He returns and directs the conversation, usually commenting on one or another of the utensils. After this formal conversation is over, the fire is smothered and the kettle is allowed to cool. Thin, weak tea is served to signal the end of the ceremony.

Some modern Japanese are guilty of paying more attention to the rules and ceremonial rituals of the tea ceremony than to its aesthetic, contemplative intent. Teahouses, or *sukiya*, are status symbols, as are hired tea masters who perform the ceremony with solemn perfection. Japanese tea schools enroll hundreds of students, both men and women desiring to learn the art form. Tea entertainments with more than two thousand people are common in Japan, events where reflection and intimacy are impossible. Nevertheless, *Cha-no-yu* lives on, and the Japanese have nothing but reverence for the idea of the ritual, even calling tea "*O Cha*," or "honorable tea."

Ginger-Honey Sponge Cake

SERVES 10 TO 12

One 2-inch-long knob fresh ginger

4 large eggs

3 large egg yolks

¾ cup granulated sugar

¼ cup honey

1½ cups sifted self-rising flour

Pinch of salt

Confectioners' sugar, for dusting

Preheat the oven to 350°F. Lighlty butter a 9-inch square baking pan. Line the bottom with wax paper or parchment paper. Flour the pan, tapping out the excess.

Peel and then grate the ginger. Put the gratings into a fine-mesh sieve set over a small bowl and press against the ginger to extract the juice. You will have about 1 tablespoon of ginger juice.

Using an electric mixer set on medium speed, beat the eggs and egg yolks until thick. Gradually add the sugar and beat until the mixture triples in volume. Still beating, slowly add the honey and ginger juice.

Whisk together the flour and salt and then fold the dry ingredients into the batter, adding them one-third at a time. Scrape the batter into the pan and bake for 30 to 35 minutes or until the cake is nicely browned and the edges pull away from the sides of the pan. Set the pan on a wire rack to cool for 20 minutes before inverting the cake onto the wire rack. Peel off the wax paper and cool the cake completely. Dust with confectioners' sugar before serving.

Note: This recipe was adapted from Elizabeth Andoh, *An American Taste of Japan* (New York: William Morrow and Company, Inc., 1985).

Essence of Green Tea Cookies

MAKES ABOUT 36 COOKIES

2 cups bleached all-purpose flour

1½ teaspoons ground ginger

½ teaspoon baking soda

¼ teaspoon salt

½ cup (1 stick) unsalted butter, at room temperature

½ cup granulated sugar

½ cup packed light brown sugar

1 large egg

1 teaspoon almond extract

3 tablespoons brewed green tea, steeped for 5 minutes and cooled

Granulated sugar, for sprinkling

In a bowl, combine the flour, ginger, baking soda, and salt and whisk 8 to 10 times.

Using an electric mixer set on medium-high speed, cream the butter until light and fluffy. Add the granulated and brown sugar and mix until combined. Add the egg and then the almond extract, mixing well. Add the tea and mix well. Cover the bowl and refrigerate for at least 1 hour.

Lay a piece of plastic wrap on a work surface and scrape the dough onto it. Using your hands and the plastic wrap as guides, form the dough into a log about 9 inches long and 2 inches in diameter. Wrap securely and refrigerate for at least 1 hour until firm.

Preheat the oven to 350°F. Lightly butter 2 baking sheets.

Unwrap the log and slice it into 1/4-inch-thick slices. Lay them on the cookie sheets, leaving about 2 inches between cookies. Sprinkle the cookies with granulated sugar and bake for about 12 minutes or until the cookies are lightly browned on the bottom. Cool for several minutes on the baking sheets and then cool completely on wire racks.

"Drinking tea stimulates the mind, keeps people awake, reduces weight, and brightens eyesight."
from *Book of Herbs*, written during the Qin/Han Dynasties

"Tea quenches thirst, relieves indigestion, clears the throat, reduces sleepiness, brightens eyesight, promotes thinking, eliminates anguish, and cuts down grease."
from *Tea Recipes* by Tsien Tsun Nien of the Ming Dynasty

"The Sage of Jade Spring loves to pick tea leaves and drink tea. At age eighty his cheeks still look like peach flowers. His tea has a light aroma and is smooth, is different from other tea, and therefore can rejuvenate the elderly."
Tang Dynasty poet Li Po

"Tea is the magical medicine for health and longevity; it grows in mountains where the soil is divine. People who pick tea live long. India and China treasure [the pickers]; in Japan, we love tea. Tea indeed is a magical medicine."
from *Note on Tea and Health* by Zen Buddhist priest Yeisei

The Health Benefits of Tea

From the earliest days of its consumption, tea has been praised for its medicinal qualities. Misty Chinese legends tell of how the first tea connoisseurs celebrated its health benefits. Confucius is credited with encouraging the Chinese to drink tea to prevent the spread of disease. Whether the wise man understood that boiling water before drinking it was a way to render it safe or whether he believed the benefits rested in the tea leaves is unknown, but the results were the same.

Many hundreds of years later the French imported tea (even earlier than the English) purely for its health benefits. Some seventeenth-century French physicians proclaimed that tea was good for nearly everything that ailed you, from rotting teeth to gout. Others decried it, saying it would lead to nothing but death! A similar debate raged

Punch and Grog

First made in France in 1653, punch has long been a tea-based drink, although in modern times any number of sweet, cold concoctions are called "punch." Punch quickly became popular at parties and in cafés in London and Rotterdam, as well as Paris. The original was mainly tea mixed with lemon, sugar, and alcohol, and dubbed bolleponche *(bowl of punch). The name has nothing to do with the wallop provided by the drink; instead, it most likely derives from the Hindustani word* panch, *meaning five. Counting the water and tea leaves, there are five ingredients in traditional punch. When ice was added, the festive drink became Roman punch; the ice reduced the alcoholic aroma and made it more appealing, it was believed, to ladies.*

Grog is a warm tea-and-rum drink favored by the British Navy. The story goes that it is named for Admiral Edward Vernon, whose nickname was "Old Grog" because of his penchant for wearing a heavy coat made of grogram, a coarse weatherproof fabric. Around 1740, the admiral ordered his crews to dilute their rum ration with water as an economy measure. The sailors discovered that the rum was more potent if the water was warm, which led to the obvious addition of tea. Given the medicinal properties of tea, which was drunk by sailors suffering from the fever, grog was considered an even better antidote to all that ailed them. Feverish sailors took a steaming cup of grog to bed with them, hanging their hats at the foot of the hammock. They drank the grog until they could "see" two hats. At that point they considered themselves cured!

in Germany, while in Holland, a country greatly dependent on the tea trade, the health benefits were embraced. In England and the New World, tea's healthful properties were also appreciated but were quickly eclipsed by its role as daily refreshment.

It is no coincidence that the hot beverages made from herbs and prescribed by doctors, midwives, and others practicing medicine in those times were called "tea." These could be called the first tisanes, although indications are they were not as tasty as today's versions. These infusions were given to people for symptoms ranging from insomnia and lack of appetite to fever and seizures. Without doubt some worked, while many more did not.

Tea was commonly drunk on British Navy ships in the eighteenth and nineteenth centuries to ward off fevers, help with conditions such as constipation, and keep sailors alert when on night watch. It also helped fight dysentery. British seafaring writer William Hutchinson praised the powers of tea in his *A Treatise on Naval Architecture*. According to Hutchinson, when a ship on which he was sailing picked up a shipment of tea in China and the crew started drinking it, he and his fellow sailors revived from the debilitating ailments that had so decimated the crew during the outgoing voyage. "It has been my custom, ever since, to drink tea, twice a day, when I could get it," he wrote.

Tea and Health Today

Doctors, research scientists, and other practitioners have in modern times studied the effects of tea on the human body. Few believe it is as powerful an agent of good health as was believed in ancient times or even in Europe in the seventeenth, eighteenth, and nineteenth centuries, but some health experts give credence to tea's preventa-tive health properties.

Over the centuries, both green and black tea have been credited with marvelous health benefits, although each type of tea is sometimes credited with different ones. This is not surprising considering the tea most commonly drunk in a country will be the tea studied: green tea in Japan; black tea in Europe or the United States. All tea comes from the same plant, *Camellia sinesis*, and consequently both black and green teas share many health benefits. However, as with such variables as taste and color, some health experts believe that how the tea is processed contributes to variables in health benefits, too.

Overall, tea is credited with strengthening capillaries, preventing atherosclerosis, lowering blood pressure, fighting some infections and cancers, destroying some bacteria, reducing the incidence of dental cavities, and maintaining the elasticity of the skin. These are big claims for a common beverage that is consumed the world over. But are they accurate?

Studies in Europe, the United States, India, Japan, China, and else-where are promising. Many show that tea may indeed possess valu-able properties that contribute to overall good health. The common wisdom is that tea is a preventative—not a cure. This is not to say its palliative powers are not considerable. Taking a cup of hot tea to bed with you, perhaps spiked with a little rum or brandy, sweetened with honey or flavored with lemon, may make you feel better, but it will not cure the common cold or the winter's flu.

The nutritional content of tea is quite rich. It has only traces of fat and calories, so these are essentially negligible. Of minerals and vitamins, it contains notable percentages of calcium (16 percent of the daily requirement), zinc (10 percent), folic acid (10 percent), vitamin B_1 (9 percent), vitamin B_2 (25 percent), and vitamin B_6 (6 percent). However, do not expect tea to meet the daily requirements for essential nutrients that can only be satisfied by a healthful and well-balanced diet.

Recent studies show the following:

Antioxidants: Tea contains natural antioxidants—even more than vitamin C or red wine—that are believed to fight cancer and other diseases.

Antiviral and antibacterial properties: Tea has properties that may inhibit common throat and stomach infections and may even help suppress influenza virus. Its antibacterial properties can also help reduce the effects of diarrhea and food poisoning.

Healthy gums and teeth: Tea inhibits tooth decay and plaque as an organic source of fluoride. It may also combat the specific bacterial activity that causes periodontal disease.

Nervous system: Black tea may stimulate the nervous system in a way that is good for heart health.

Cholesterol and heart disease: Green tea has been credited with helping to lower cholesterol and helps lower the risk of heart disease.

Stroke prevention: The high flavonoid content in black tea is said to help prevent stroke.

Skin damage: Green tea appears to protect the skin from sun damage and the consequent signs of aging.

Postmenopausal protection: Black tea may inhibit some cancers that affect postmenopausal women.

Zinc: Tea is a rich source of zinc, an essential mineral that boosts our immune systems, helps prevent some cancers and blindness in old age, and fights colds. Zinc also helps maintain our senses of smell, taste, and vision.

Calcium: Relatively high amounts of calcium, a mineral that is essential for life because it helps build strong bones, are found in tea. It is important in fighting osteoporosis, high blood pressure, high cholesterol, and arthritis.

B-complex vitamins B_1, B_2, and B_6: Vitamin B_1 (thiamin) is essential for heart health. In the extreme, thiamin deficiencies lead to beriberi, a fatal condition. B_1 improves mental abilities, controls anemia, and can help control diabetes. Vitamin B_2 (riboflavin) protects against free-radical damage and contributes to general energy levels. It also protects against some cancers and against anemia. Vitamin B_6 is an overall immunity booster, helps control diabetes, prevents some skin diseases, and soothes nervous disorders.

Folic acid: This compound is essential to the metabolic processes of the body. Specifically, it helps prevent some cancers and can help in the treatment of atherosclerosis.

Black tea is associated more often with preventing strokes than is green tea. Other health claims associated with black tea (as well as green tea) are its antioxidant capabilities because of the high occurrence of flavonoids. Flavonoids are vitaminlike compounds found in some fruits and vegetables as well as tea. The result is protection against some cancers.

The presence of theophyline, an alkaloid present in low concentration in black tea, may stimulate the nervous system while "relaxing" the blood vessels and consequently may help the heart to work better. The folic acid in black tea may also contribute to the formation of blood cells, which is important to a healthy body. Darjeeling and Assam teas are the teas richest in folic acid.

There is evidence to suggest that cancers of the digestive tract and the urinary tract are inhibited by black tea, as are some other cancers that particularly effect postmenopausal women. Additionally, black tea may inhibit the development of skin cancer.

When it comes to the mouth, black tea does more than please our taste buds. The vitamin B_2 found in tea contributes to mouth, lip, and tongue health (and eye health also), even while it promotes healthful, glowing skin. The relatively large amounts of fluoride found in black tea prevent tooth decay.

Green tea appears to prevent cardiovascular disease because of its cholesterol-lowering capabilities. This may be due to natural lipid-lowering ingredients in green tea called catechins. This group of compounds contained in the tea leaves lowers absorption of cholesterol and may even promote its expulsion from the body.

Green tea has been credited with helping in the treatment of abdominal, intestinal, and cerebral hemorrhage, and the prevention of capillary fragility and the formation of bladder stones. It is also found to help in the treatment of nephritis (inflammation of the kidney), chronic hepatitis, hypertension, and induced leukemia. Green tea may modify inflammation in cases of rheumatism and chronic hepatitis. It also has been shown, in some studies, to help with the long-term control of atherosclerosis and hypertension. It may help prevent serious complications from cerebral hemorrhage and myocardial infarction.

As useful as green tea may be for heart health and associated problems, its possible cancer-prevention capabilities should not be overlooked. The polyphenols in green tea may help fight cancers of the lung, stomach, esophagus, duodenum, pancreas, liver, and colon.

What About Caffeine?

There is no question that high amounts of caffeine adversely affect some people. Risks range from insomnia and upset stomach to increased breathing rates and rapid heartbeats. Some people become jittery and irritable with too much caffeine and may even suffer from anxiety attacks. On the other hand, caffeine can increase alertness, focus thought processes, quell headaches, and promote a mild sense of well-being.

Caffeine is a naturally occurring substance found in the leaves, seeds, or fruits of more than sixty plants. The most common of these are coffee beans, chocolate beans, and tea leaves. Most doctors agree that moderate tea and coffee drinkers have little cause for alarm when it comes to caffeine consumption. This translates to two cups of coffee a day or four or five cups of tea.

The caffeine content in a six-ounce cup of brewed black tea is 55 to 70 milligrams, while in the same size cup of coffee, it ranges from 100 to 150 milligrams. Green and oolong teas have less caffeine than black tea; green teas, about a third as much, and oolongs, about two-thirds as much. Every now and then you will read that a pound of tea contains far more caffeine than a pound of coffee. This is true, but consider that from a pound of coffee you can brew about forty cups, while a pound of tea yields as many as two hundred cups.

Who Should Not Drink Tea

Fortunately, most people the world over can drink tea happily and healthfully. I would be remiss, however, if I did not mention situations in which tea drinking can be counter-productive to health.

Lactating mothers: Tea-drinking can reduce the secretion of milk. This does not apply to pregnant women unless they are otherwise advised by their doctors. The zinc in tea can be beneficial to them.

Children: I don't think it's a good idea to let children under the age of ten drink tea because, in concentrated amounts, the tannins can combine with proteins in the intestines and stunt growth. Caffeine is not much of an issue with kids, who eliminate it twice as rapidly as adults.

When We Should Not Drink Tea

Right before a meal: Drinking tea directly before eating can dilute gastric juices necessary for good digestion.

With medication: Tea's natural compounds can inhibit the effectiveness of some medications and may contribute to harmful side effects. Check with your doctor.

Before sleeping: The natural caffeine content of tea may interfere with sleep. Of course, tisanes such as chamomile enhance sleep.

Glossary

Agony of the leaves: The unfolding of the leaves when boiling water is poured over them.

Aroma: The tea's odor, either of the infused leaf or the steeped result. Typically, a tea's aroma is likened to a flower or fruit.

Astringency: The quality of the tea's liquor that gives a bite or piquancy to the taste.

Bakey: An unpleasant taste caused by firing tea leaves at a temperature that is too high, resulting in the leaves losing too much moisture. Not as bad as "burnt."

Biscuity: A pleasant quality usually associated with Assam teas.

Bite: The astringency that imparts a sought-after quality to black teas.

Bitter: An unpleasantly biting taste that usually results from oversteeping teas.

Black: A dark, brown-black leaf, characteristic of a fully fermented leaf.

Blackish: A quality associated with carefully sorted CTC tea leaves.

Bloom: The sheen on black leaf tea, the result of minimal handling during sorting and processing. Unlike with chocolate, tea bloom is desirable.

Body: The viscosity or strength of the liquor, which can be full, light, moderate, and so on.

Brassy: An undesirable tangy or metallic taste, indicating leaves that have not been properly withered during processing.

Bright: A sparkling characteristic of all fine teas' liquors.

Brisk: A lively, pleasant trait associated with all fine black teas.

Brown: The result of the harsh treatment of CTC tea leaves, resulting in flat, brown-looking leaves.

Burnt: The undesirable taste of leaves that have been overfired during processing.

Character: A positive quality of well-harvested leaves, usually grown at altitudes between four thousand and seven thousand feet.

Chesty: The resinous odor or taste of tea that has been packed in chests made from uncured wood or another inferior material.

Chunky: An extra-large, broken tea leaf.

Clean: A leaf that is free of extraneous fiber, dust, twigs, and other debris.

Coarse: A harsh, unpleasant taste.

Colory: The depth of color and strength of tea.

Common: An indistinctly flavored liquor, usually thin, light, and without body, and made from poor-quality tea leaves.

Complex: The perfect mêlange of various flavors and aromas coming together to make an appealing tea.

Crepey: The crimped, crepelike appearance characteristic of OP (Orange Pekoe) teas.

CTC: A process of cutting, tearing, and curling tea leaves, which results in full-bodied teas made from leaves that may not be of the highest quality (but not of low quality, either).

Curly: The curling appearance of some whole-leaf teas.

Dry: Tea leaves that are overfired and dry, but are neither burnt nor bakey.

Dull: A tea leaf lacking in gloss or sheen.

Earthy: A term used to describe a certain earthy flavor of some teas. This is usually the result of the soil and other growing conditions in a particular tea-growing region, which is not necessarily undesirable, or the result of improper storage in a damp place.

Even: A tea whose leaves are uniform in size and appearance.

Flaky: Can refer to leaves that break and crumble easily, which is undesirable.

Flat: Soft tea lacking in bite and briskness.

Flavor: A highly desirable trait and usually the result of teas grown at altitudes between four thousand and seven thousand feet.

Fruity: A piquant characteristic of oolongs and other teas.

Full: A good combination of color and strength. May not indicate briskness, but does denote a round, smooth mouthfeel.

Gone off: A term to describe tea that has spoiled because of poor storage, bad packing, or because it has turned stale.

Grainy: The primary grades of the best CTC teas.

Gray: The color of the leaves caused by too much abrasion during sorting.

Green: Refers to black and oolong teas that are underfermented or to leaves plucked from immature bushes. This has nothing to do with green teas, which are a type of tea.

Hard: An especially pungent brew.

Harsh: Unpleasantly rough-tasting tea that has not been properly withered.

Heavy: A thick, strong liquor without the accompanying briskness.

Lacking: A liquor without body or other strong characteristics.

Leafy: Teas with large, long leaves.

Light: A leaf of light weight.

Make: Tea that perfectly matches its stated grade.

Malty: An underlying flavor usually associated with Assam tea.

Mature: A tea that is neither flat nor bitter.

Metallic: Tea with a sharp, almost coppery taste.

Muddy: A dull liquor lacking in lightness or brightness.

Muscatel: This is a flavor most often associated with Darjeelings and refers to the flavor of the muscat grapes, which are the grapes used to make muscatel wine.

Neat: A grade of tea with good "make" and well-sized leaves.

Nose: The smell of the dry tea leaf.

Ordinaire: A term for a good, standard quality of tea.

Peak: The apex of black-tea tasting—green and oolong teas do not peak. Peak occurs a few moments after the liquor enters the mouth and the tea's qualities are experienced.

Pekoe: The larger of the two leaves on the shoot of a fine plucking. Pekoe or Orange Pekoe is the name for the standard blend of tea sold in the United States.

Plain: A tea that is clean-tasting but lacks enlivening traits.

Pointy: A liquor with one or more positive characteristics.

Powdery: Fine tea dust and not desirable.

Pungent: A good combination of strength, briskness, and brightness.

Quality: The characteristics of a cup of tea.

Ragged: Tea that tastes uneven and looks dull because of poor processing.

Self-drinking: A tea with enough good characteristics such as aroma, body, flavor, and color that it can be enjoyed without blending it with other teas.

Smoky: A desirable characteristic of some Chinese teas, especially Lapsang Souchong. When found in other teas, it is undesirable.

Soft: Unremarkable flavor caused by poor firing during fermentation.

Stale: Faded aroma and "dead" flavor caused by excessive age and the subsequent lack of quality.

Stalk and fiber: Residues of the tea plant that are usually part of low-grade teas, reflecting poor sorting practices.

Stewed: Tea that tastes bitter because it has been steeped too long or because it is made from poorly fired leaves.

Taint: A flavor that invades the tea leaves, usually caused by storing the tea too near food or something else with a strong odor.

Tarry: A desirable smoky flavor caused by smoking tea with wood or charcoal. This is most commonly associated with Lapsang Souchong.

Thick: A richly colored infusion.

Thin: A weak-colored infusion lacking in any strong or desirable characteristics.

Tip: The youngest leaf on the plant growing directly below the bud.

Tippy: A term describing dry leaf tea and indicating high-quality tea in terms of manufacturing.

Toasty: A desirable characteristic of fine Keemuns and other highly fired teas.

Uneven: Leaves with gradations of color.

Weedy: Thin black teas; also refers to green teas with a vegetable-like aroma.

Well twisted: A fully withered leaf that is rolled tightly lengthwise.

Winey: A desirable quality in some teas, particularly Keemun and Darjeeling.

Woody: A synonym for weedy.

Suggested Readings

Andoh, Elizabeth. *An American Taste of Japan*. New York: William Morrow and Company, Inc., 1985.

Burgess, Anthony. *The Book of Tea* (preface). New York: Abbeville Press, 1992.

Evans, John C. *Tea in China*. New York: Greenwood Press, 1992.

Fleming, Thomas. *Liberty! An American Revolution*. New York: Viking Penguin, 1997.

Manchester, Carole. *French Tea*. New York: Hearst Books, 1993.

———. *Tea in the East*. New York: Hearst Books, 1996.

Norman, Jill. *Teas & Tisanes*. New York: Bantam Books, 1989.

Ortiz, Elisabeth Lambert. *The Encyclopedia of Herbs, Spices & Flavorings*. New York: Dorling Kindersley, Inc., 1994.

Pettigrew, Jane. *The Tea Companion*. New York: Macmillan, 1997.

Pratt, James Norwood. *The Tea Lovers Companion*. New York: Birch Lane Press, 1995.

Sadler, A. L. *Cha-No-Yu*. Rutland, Vt.: Charles E. Tuttle Company, Inc., 1994.

Victoria magazine. *The Charms of Tea*. New York: *Hearst Books*, 1991.

Index

About the Author

Tomislav Podreka is founder of serendipitea, one of the largest independent importers of fine and specialty teas in the United States. He is the education chairman of the American Premium Tea Institute. A popular speaker on the history and philosophy of tea, he travels across the country lecturing and giving tea tastings. He lives in Connecticut.

For more information about serendipitea contact:
www.serendipitea.com